No Thanks, I'm On A Budget!

: a beginner's guide to developing healthy money habits to budget, save, and eliminate debt!

Written by

ALICIA GAGE

Disclaimer:

The content of this book is for informational and educational purposes about personal finance only. The information provided is intended to offer advice, but it may not apply directly to your personal financial situation. The information presented are recommendations. All recommendations are made without guarantee from the author. The author disclaim any liability, loss, or risk in connection with the use of this information. The information provided was last updated in 2020. There may be new economic and financial changes that may affect the content of this book. As each individual situation is unique, please consult a professional before making any important financial decisions.

Contents

ACKNOWLEDGMENTS

First and foremost, I would like to give honor to God for giving me the vision, strength, wisdom, and knowledge.
-Jeremiah 29:11

I would like to thank my brother, Anton Gage, for his encouragement and support through this whole process. Your kind words, day in and day out, truly motivated me to push through.

I would also like to thank my mother, Elizabeth Hart. Thank you for supporting me with this book.

LET ME TELL YOU A STORY…

Finally, 2011!

It was a new year and Sasha was feeling pretty good about the way her life has been going. She was entering into her 2nd semester of graduate school. She was working at a bank and twice a week at a local dry cleaner. Her finances were in order. She was very proud of the progress she had been making with her savings and emergency fund account. With two jobs, Sasha was able to pay all of her bills with just one check and place the rest into her savings account. On top of that, Sasha was back in the 750-credit score club. She created different strategies to eliminate debt that she consumed while in college which allowed her to go from being classified as a "risky" borrower to becoming a "very good" borrower in the eyes of creditors. At 23 years old, Sasha was single, had her own place, few bills, and a working car that was paid in full.

Sasha was always a giving person so during this time, it was so easy for her to say yes to those who came to her for a loan. She felt amazing being able to accept invitations to brunch and enjoy a night out on the town with friends every now and then without having to worry about going over her monthly budget. She was doing well, and in her eyes, this was the perfect definition of being independent.

Her only goal at the time was to become a full-time employee at the bank and later get promoted so she could put her master's degree in finance to use. She dedicated her time to learn new things and took on additional tasks just so management would see just how much she wanted to get promoted. Life is great right now, or is it?

Two months later, she got word from her supervisor at the bank that there was a change in her scheduled hours.

"Here is your schedule for the week." Her supervisor hands her the sheet of paper.

Looking over the paper, she asks, "Why am I only working 23 hours again this week? And working yet another Saturday? It's not fair that I have to work every Saturday."

Her supervisor replies, "Well, we replaced the full-time position with two part-time positions, so now your hours will decrease. And as far as Saturday, well something drastic must happen, like death in the family for you to get a Saturday off."

Sasha looks back at the paper and says, "When I asked you about this last month, you specifically told me my hours would not be affected, but now it is? How did I go from working about 35 hours a week to only 20? And this whole Saturday thing, I don't think it's fair. That is not what I signed up for."

Her supervisor replied with, "Well technically, you are part-time so your hours can be as low as 20. That's how it is going to be. I'll *try* to give you more hours, but as for this week, that's all we can give you."

"Okay, thanks." Sasha says sadly as she walks away.

A few months following that incident, she receives another check that didn't reflect her usual payout. "$480-how could this be?" she says to herself. Her first check of the month usually covered the majority of her bills, but now she would have to use both checks just to pay rent. The money she loaned was never returned and her car was now acting up. One day while driving along I-26, the speed meter on the dashboard of her car started acting funny. The miles went from 60 to 40, and then down to 0. Sasha began pushing hard on the gas, but it never went back to 60. She was stuck on the side of the road on a hot day in July. Once she was able to, she had the car repaired. A new fuel pump, a new transmission part, and even a brand-new battery. $200 here, $350 there. Swiping her credit card left and right just to fix problem after problem. She had to call the bank twice to ask for a credit increase just so she wouldn't max out her credit card. Weeks later, as she was on her way to work, the car wouldn't start. Sasha later called the mechanic and sighed as she listened to him express how this time she needed a new alternator.

With that came the unwanted advice from those close to her: *Maybe you should just get another car, You definitely need to get a new car. You work at a bank; you should be able to get a good interest rate on an auto loan.* Everyone had an opinion of what she needed to do, yet she had no idea of how any of that would happen. She was barely paying rent and a new car note would only hurt her finances more. At this point, instead of depositing money into her emergency fund account, it was now going into the account she used to pay bills.

Sasha knew the basis of budgeting. She was very good at saving, but things had changed and now, after completing her monthly budget, she only had $100 left for food and gas. This was impossible to live off, especially since she didn't know about couponing at the time. So, ramen noodles, spaghetti, and grilled cheese sandwiches became her best friends.

Sasha logged in to her online banking almost every day and the only thing she saw was transfer, withdrawal, transfer, withdrawal from her savings account. She even got a letter from the bank stating that if she continued with this behavior, they would switch her savings account to a checking account. Not only did her credit score decrease again, but her bills increased as well. Although she was only making minimum payments on her credit cards, the payments increased from $30 to $150. The lease on her apartment was increasing because it was time for her to renew. With school coming up in a few weeks, Sasha had to figure out how she was going to pay for books. To make matters worse, Sasha got very sick which caused her to rack up thousands of dollars in medical bills.

To bring in more income, she applied for jobs in the finance, accounting, and banking industry. She applied for entry-level accountant and financial representative positions, but, unfortunately, every position she applied for was rejected. Her undergraduate degree in finance and experience as a teller wasn't helping her move into a higher position in retail banking either.

"Thank you for your application. Based on criteria, you are not qualified for this position."

"Thank you for your interest. We found someone more suitable for this position."

"Your resume looks great. Your interview skills are excellent. You have achieved a lot at a very young age; however, you are overqualified for this position."

Sasha couldn't believe she was being rejected like this. She applied to over 50 jobs, took about 15 job assessments, and had over 10 in person and telephone interviews. Interview after interview went by and she was either over or under qualified. She was tired of going to interviews. She was only trying to make ends meet but kept getting rejected. Her checks were still a whopping $480 every two weeks and yet again she would have to drive her mom's blue dodge caravan, which was also her stepdad's work truck from time to time, just to get to school and work.

That routine lasted for a few more months until she finally found another job. Although this job wasn't what she needed to replenish her finances, she made it work. The new job was still a part-time position but it paid more than what she was currently making. At this point, her savings account was on the verge of becoming completely depleted. 2012 was approaching and she saw no signs of improvement. Confused and not sure of what to do, Sasha was at a lost, hoping things would get better.

INTRODUCTION

Hi, my name is Alicia Gage and the story you just read is about me. I wanted to share with you how quickly things can change in your life financially. At 23, I thought I had everything in order with my finances. I thought I was going to get an increase in income, maintain my high 750 credit score, get a better job because of my degree, then life happened. My income decreased and I couldn't find a job for months to help pay the bills. I was headed in a bad place financially, but if it wasn't for my emergency fund, my situation could've been worse.

My past experience, both personal and professional, in the banking industry has not only taught me to love finance but to help individuals learn about financial literacy as well. Finance is something that's a part of everyone's life, yet people fail to understand or even want to know about it.

This is why I wrote this book. I would recommend this book for anyone who is in the beginning stages of learning about finances or in the process of rebuilding themselves financially. I want people to learn from my story so they will know what to do should they experience a decline in their finances. I was lucky to teach myself about saving at a very young age, due to my past mistakes in college, and now I want to be able to teach you as well.

This book is designed for those who have found it difficult to budget, save, and eliminate debt. If you find yourself constantly withdrawing from savings, unable to pay bills the way you would like, or wanting to become financially stable, then this book is for you. My objective is to make sure you gain a better relationship with money. This process first begins with a budget, which is what you will be learning about. The time is now to make better financial decisions for you and your family.

No matter what your situation is, it is always imperative that you understand finance and prepare for the future now. I understood the true definition of what "saving for a rainy day" was back in 2011, and now I want everyone to understand this phrase as well.

The tips and strategies you are about to receive through this book has helped me to rebuild my savings, improve my credit score, pay my car off early, eliminate credit card debt, and maximize earnings through investing. Grab a pen and use the notes section located at the end of this book. It's time for you to learn about personal finance!

CHAPTER 1

WHAT DOES PERSONAL FINANCE MEAN TO YOU?

When I think of what personal finance means, I think of it in its simplest terms; understanding your financial health, becoming aware of financial activities, and creating strategies that will help to achieve financial stability.

Learning about personal finance enables you to budget, save money, and eliminate debt. This in turn, will help you to maintain a high credit score, build generational wealth, form ways to increase personal net worth, and allow you to do the things you love to do.

Many individuals dislike this topic because it can be very confusing, frustrating, and hard to understand. Some feel like they are too far gone. Some feel that they are already in a bad financial situation and it's too late to achieve financial freedom.

Financial health isn't something that can be swept under the rug and left unaddressed. Preventive measures should be taken with finances, much like that of your physical health. This is how you develop financial freedom and success.

Let's review your personal goals and define what personal finance means to you. In the section below, write out your thoughts.

_____

_____

_____

_____

_____

_____

_____

_____

_____

_____

_____

_____

_____

_____

_____

_____

_____

_____

_____

_____

First and foremost, to begin understanding personal finance, it is necessary to understand budgeting. Budgeting is defined as "An estimate of income and expenditures for a set period of time". Think of it more as a simple organization and prioritization of cash flow; a stepping stone to becoming financially successful.

Many of us want to have better credit scores, build generational wealth, and retire at an acceptable age, however, we are not organizing our finances as such to achieve these goals. Some people want to bypass the budgeting process. It can't be avoided. Without a budget, you cannot achieve financial success. Money mismanagement is the predicted outcome if one does not do the research required to maintain financial stability.

Try taking a different approach to the idea of budgeting. Think of budgeting as a newly planted tree that will eventually grow. The tree starts as a seed that grows over time, with the proper nurturing of rich soil, water, and sunlight. In this case, the seed represents the budget. Once the seed begins to grow, the trunk, branches, and leaves begins to grow. This represents your personal financial goals. When you have the foundation of budgeting in place, all of your financial goals become relatively easy to achieve.

Today, many individuals are trying to "secure the bag" so to speak and failing at organizing their finances. Earning money with a plan to use it wisely will ensure that your hard work is not wasted through maintaining better spending habits. It's best to always prioritize and understand the importance of budgeting.

Having worked in the banking industry for many years, I discovered that there was a lack of basic financial literacy. I witnessed a trend of many unnecessary events, such as outstanding fees due to negative balances, customers with no savings accounts, and customers applying for credit that they did not necessarily need.

I also realized that throughout my own life, I was never taught about basic financial literature until I had to experience it on my own. Before, I was never taught about good debt versus bad debt, how to eliminate debt effectively, and the benefits of budgeting. It wasn't until my Junior year of college when financial literature became an important aspect of my life.

I am pretty sure at this point you are asking yourself, well how do I create a budget? The next chapter will provide 7 simple steps to creating a budget. Don't forget your pen and the note section located at the end of this book.

CHAPTER 2

7 STEPS TO CREATING A BUDGET

Before you know the 7 steps to creating a budget, first think about how you budget. How do you organize your finances each month?

_____

_____

_____

_____

_____

_____

_____

_____

_____

_____

_____

_____

_____

_____

_____

_____

_____

_____

I'm assuming that many of you may have wrote:

1. I check my bank account and it shows me how much I've spent/ have left (I use my banks budgeting tracker)
2. I don't budget/ I don't know how to budget.
3. I budget but always end up going over my budget each month/I'm not sure how high expenses are supposed to be.

These are the most common responses when asked about budgeting. Checking your bank account is great, but it doesn't help or show where you are financially. It only shows how you spend your money. Also, your budget may not be working for you because you have too many expenses and not enough income based on your current living conditions. If you are having problems in organizing your monthly income and expenses, or simply do not know how to budget, these next 7 simple steps will help to better your financial strategy.

1.   Create a list of all sources of income for the month

The first step to creating a budget is to list all sources of income for the month. This includes weekly or monthly paychecks from your job, social security benefits, pensions, child support, alimony, etc. When listing income, *NEVER* include any anticipated income. For example, if you loaned your friend $200.00 and they stated they would pay you back, or if you are expecting to receive a refund check, never include this as income because you may never receive it. It could hurt your budget if you anticipated using the $200.00 you loaned to a friend to pay your electricity bill, and never got paid back. When the anticipated money does come, you should place it into your savings account, pay a debtor, or use it towards a financial goal.

Considering the individuals who have unpredictable income or fluctuating income, such as a waiter or car salesman, I recommend doing a trend analysis of your yearly bank statements from the previous year or two and base your monthly budget from that. For example, waiters should expect more income during the summer months because this is the time when more tourists are around (at least this is what happens in my area). If you are self- employed, I would recommend that you pay yourself on a weekly, bi-weekly, or monthly basis, if you don't already. Create a payroll strategy as if you were working for someone else.

Step 1: List all sources of income for the month

1.

2.

3.

4.

5.

2. __Create a list of all fixed expenses for the month__

Once you have a list of all sources of income for the month, you will need to list all fixed expenses for the month. This includes monthly expenses such as rent/mortgage, transportation, utilities, and other needed expenses. Now, the expenses does not end here. In this section, you would also include a budget for food, gas (for your car), and _SAVINGS!_ I know you may be thinking, "Really? A food budget?" I get this reaction with my clients most of the time.

Let me explain. Typically, individuals only budget for regular expenses (rent, water, utilities, etc.) and whatever is left, they use for food, gas, savings, and regular spending. Generally, what happens is individuals continuously swipe their debit cards until they have almost depleted the account for food, gas, and other spending. When the account becomes fully depleted, individuals then make excuses for the reasons why they are stretching their accounts thin. This in turn makes the account go into a negative status and individuals must turn to credit cards, loans, and savings accounts to fund other expenditures until the next paycheck. It's a continuous cycle that only results in more debt and less opportunity to gain financial freedom. Therefore, having a food, gas, and savings budget is important.

Below is a list of fixed expenses that you may have. Keep in my mind that you should always list your basic living necessities first. (_Food, rent/mortgage, water, utilities, transportation, and savings_)

Rent/Mortgage

Water

Electricity/Utility

Trash/Sewer

Phone

Loans/Credit Cards/Lines of Credit

Childcare/Daycare/School expenses

Cable

Internet

Security system/Identity theft protection

Pet care

Transportation

Insurance

Monthly subscriptions (apple music, Netflix, gym, hobby dues, etc.)

Food/Groceries

Savings/Retirement accounts/Investment accounts

Tithes/Offering/Charity

Legal fees/Legal obligations

Therapy/Counseling

Medical expenses

Toiletries

Laundry/Dry cleaners

Routine home maintenance

Routine car maintenance

Taxes

Step 2: List all fixed expenses for the month

1.

2.

3.

4.

5.

6.

7.

8.

9.

10.

11.

12.

13.

14.

15.

16.

17.

18.

19.

20.

3.   <u>Create a list of all discretionary (variable) expenses for the month</u>

Once you've listed all fixed expenses, then list items for regular spending. These items should go after your fixed expenses to make sure your high priority financial responsibilities are handled first. This section should include personal items such clothes and shoes. Ladies, I know you want to buy the whole skin care line and guys like getting a great deal on shoes too, but it is important to set a limit. You must ensure that you're not overspending on luxury items when the focus should be on achieving financial success.

Make a list of everything you can think of that falls into the category of regular spending such as annual renewal fees, extra-curricular after school activities for children, and monthly self-care activities to avoid overspending. Make it a habit to include everything you spend money on. Below is an unexhausted list of other expenses that are commonly missed when creating a budget that should be included.

-Kids activities

-Family activities

-Work activities

-Organization activities

-Birthday celebrations

-Fees (application, annual)

-Monthly self-care

-Personal hobbies

-Entertainment

-Supplies (school, home)

-Clothes/Shoes expenses

-Money borrowed

Step 3: List all discretionary (variable) expenses for the month

1.

2.

3.

4.

5.

6.

7.

8.

9.

10.

11.

12.

13.

14.

15.

4. <u>Subtract expenses from income-follow the zero-based budgeting theory</u>

The next step is to subtract expenses from income, whether it is fixed or discretionary. The objective is to create a zero-based budget, meaning expenses from income should equal zero. This ensures that you know how your money is being spent each month. If the amount is negative (more expenses than income), then you have a negative cash flow. If you do have a negative cash flow, don't worry, the next section and throughout this book will help you solve this problem. The objective is to try to eliminate as many expenses as you can to get a zero-based budget.

Income=

- Expenses=

Total: 0

5. <u>Readjust budget/ follow the financial rules of thumb/ eliminate expenses</u>

Now here comes the tricky part. Readjusting your budget to achieve financial success can be difficult, hard, and confusing. For example, do you have more money going towards clothes and shoes versus your savings account? Have you included a financial goal? Do you have a portion of your income going towards retirement?

Living paycheck to paycheck without achieving any financial goals is very common, but the end result is a continual cycle of living paycheck to paycheck. This means that you will constantly live day to day without getting ahead financially because you are not achieving any monthly financial goals.

In the financial world, there are several financial rules of thumb which many financial experts have invented to help individuals understand how high expenses should be. They provide specific instructions to ensure individuals accomplish their financial goals and live within their means based on current income. Here are a few financial rules that I have found useful to help achieve financial success:

Car Loans:

- If you have a car note, it should be no more than 15% of your monthly take home pay (net pay). For example, if your take home pay is $2000 a month, your car note should not exceed $300 a month.

- The total amount of your car should not exceed your salary. You should not finance a 2021 Nissan Maxima worth about $36,000 if your income is only $30,000.

- Avoid 72-84 months auto loan terms. Although the payments are lower, you will pay more interest over the life of the loan compared to a shorter term.

- If you find a cheap car that's in good quality, consider purchasing that vehicle instead. For example, during the period of 2008-2010, I did not have a car note which allowed me to put more money into a savings account.

28/36 rule of debt ratio (for gross income):

- Household expenses should be no more than 28% of your monthly pay (combined income if more than one provider in the home) and the total household debt should be no more than 36% of your total monthly pay. This means that your monthly household payment (this includes payments within your home mortgage-principal, interest, insurance, etc.) should be no more than 28% of your gross income and the total amount of debt (including car loans, student loans, etc.), should be no more than 36%. This rule is commonly used by many loan officers to determine if you qualify for a mortgage, car, etc. They want to ensure that your debt-to-income ratio is not too high.

50/30/20 rule: (I highly recommend- also known as 50/20/30 rule-Popularized by Senator Elizabeth

Warren)

- 50% of your income should go toward necessities such as housing expenses and bills. (This includes food and gas)

- 30% of your income should go towards dining and entertainment costs (regular spending)

- 20% of your income should go towards financial goals (eliminating debt, saving, retirement, emergency fund, investments, etc.)

*Although I highly recommend this financial rule of thumb, I advise that you switch the 30% and 20% rules around. The objective is to achieve financial success, by making sure you're contributing more towards your financial responsibilities versus regular spending. I highly recommend using 30% of your income towards financial goals and only 20% towards regular spending. This will help you to achieve your financial goals much faster. Eliminating 50% of housing expenses is something to consider as well. The less you spend on expenses, the more you have to save and eliminate debt.

Snowball Method: (Popularized by personal finance expert Dave Ramsey)

- The snowball method suggests focusing on one debt at a time, starting with the smallest. Once the smallest debt is paid, you continue paying the same amount to the next smallest debt, until eventually you are debt free. Below is an example.

Phase 1:

Debt A: pay as much as you can each month until the debt is paid off.

Debt B: only pay the minimum balance

Debt C: only pay the minimum balance

Phase 2:

Debt A: PAID!

Debt B: pay the minimum balance + the amount used to eliminate Debt A

Debt C: pay the minimum balance

Phase 3:

Debt A: PAID!

Debt B: PAID!

Debt C: pay the minimum balance + the amount used to eliminate Debt A +the amount used to eliminate Debt B

- There is another concept called the avalanche method that focuses on paying the higher interest rate debt(s) first. I would only recommend this method if you have loans with extremely high interest rates. This method helps to eliminate the high cost of fees associated with the loan. It helps to eliminate the cost of compound interest.

3-6 Months Emergency Fund Rule:

- The emergency fund rule goes hand in hand with the 28/36 rule and the 50/30/20 rule. When you begin working on your financial goals, the first step is to build a savings account. If you don't have a savings account now, I highly recommend that you create a budget and make this your #1 priority. Consider saving at least $1000.00 - $2000.00 first. Once you have at least $1000.00-$2000.00 in a savings account, create a strategy (budget) that will allow you to have 3 - 6 months' worth of income available in an emergency savings account. This account should be used for ***emergency purposes only***. Situations such as losing a job or a decrease in income are a few examples.

- 10%-15% of income should go towards retirement:

  ➤ Time flies when you're having fun! You can be 20 one day and then in a few years celebrating your 40th birthday! Saving for retirement is essential if you want to retire at an acceptable age. It's not good to be 70 years old saying, "Would you like to add fries for an extra $1.49?" just because you didn't save for retirement.

  ➤ Social security benefits is one source of income for retirement, however, it should not be your only source of income after you retire. It's wise to start investing in 401(k) plans, IRA's, and other retirement accounts now. Your older self will thank your younger self in the future.

  ➤ Although retirement is important, make sure you are handling debt first. In the beginning stages, you want to make sure you are not putting too much in retirement that makes you unable to handle other financial responsibilities first. Over time, as your income increases and the amount of debt decreases, you can gradually contribute 10% or more towards retirement.

Pay Yourself First Strategy:

- Have you ever heard of the phrase pay yourself first? What do you think about when you hear this phrase? Many assume that it means to buy whatever you want, but it actually means investing in yourself first in terms of savings and building your personal financial net worth before thinking about paying anyone else. Before paying the cable company, did you deposit a set amount into your savings account? Before letting a friend borrow money, did you make a contribution to your 401(k) or IRA? Having a pay yourself first strategy ensures that your expenses are not the cause for not achieving financial success. It helps to allocate income correctly to prepare for life uncertainties. It is always important to take care of yourself first. You should always put your fixed expenses before any discretionary expenses.

Readjust Your Budget

Step 4: List readjusted expenses (fixed and discretionary)

1.

2.

3.

4.

5.

6.

7.

8.

9.

10.

11.

12.

13.

14.

15.

16.

17.

18.

19.

20.

21.

22.

23.

24.

25.

26.

27.

28.

29.

30.

6. Recalculate expenses from income

The next step is like step 3. In this step, you are going to subtract your newly readjusted expenses from your income. The objective is to minimize personal expenses as much as possible and increase the amount of funds going towards your financial goals. (Increase personal net worth)

Income=

-Expenses =

   Total: 0

7. WRITE OUT YOUR BUDGET and Stick to the Plan

The final step in creating a budget is writing it out and sticking to the plan you've created. When you write out your monthly budget, you need to sort out your financial obligations according to how you get paid. The average individual gets paid twice a month. Divide your bills accordingly to separate your expenses as such.

For some, this task is easy because bills are due at different times of the month. For others, all bills may be due at the first of the month. For situations like this, you need to decide what works best for you. Here's an example: if all bills are due on the first of the month, use your first paycheck strictly for bills and your other paycheck strictly for food, gas, savings, and personal spending. This means that you must be cautious on how you spend money on food, gas, and regular spending because you only get that "allowance" once a month.

Changing your payment due date with debtors or paying ahead of time can help organize your budget. You can also split payments. Since rent and mortgage payments are usually the largest, for example, separate it so it won't exhaust all of your funds from one paycheck.

I emphasized the phrase "***WRITE OUT YOUR BUDGET***" because this is a very important step in the process of eliminating debt and living within your set budget. As previously stated, many of us use bank apps to see our "budget" status, but the app is not showing you the proper way to budget. If you don't prefer to write, there are many budgeting apps such as: Mint, Fudget, Every Dollar, and Clarity Money, just to name a few. If this is your first-time budgeting, I highly recommend writing it on paper first. Get a planner or small notebook and keep it with you at all times. I also have a budget planner available on my website, www.aliciasfinancialcorner.com, that will help in organizing your monthly budget.

Set a time or day to look over your budget to make sure you are sticking to the plan. Personally, I prefer to track my expenses every morning. I use Sunday afternoon to check my progress and set limits for the next week to stay on track. However you decide, just make sure you keep track. Below, you will find a spreadsheet that will help keep you on track. (This spreadsheet is for income and expenses recorded on a bi-weekly basis).

Check #1: Total Income:	Paid?	Budgeted Amount	Actual Amount	Difference
List of Expenses:				
1				
2				
3				
4				
5				
6				
7				
8				
9				
10				
11				
12				
Check #2: Total Income:				
List of Expenses:				
1				
2				
3				
4				
5				
6				
7				
8				
9				
10				
11				
12				
Total:				

CHAPTER 3

WHY BUDGETS FAIL AND HOW TO PREVENT FAILURE

Now that have a better understanding of how to create a monthly budget, I want to dive deeper into the issues that come with budgeting. Many of us have a budget, but by the end of the month, it's a failed plan. Funds are withdrawn from savings accounts, credit cards are being swiped, or we end up falling short on funds to pay the rest of our bills. As stated before, budgeting can be very hard, confusing, and frustrating. Success doesn't happen overnight. From personal experience, it took me months before I became better at minimizing expenses and overcoming bad financial habits.

The next section will talk about why budgets fail and how to prevent it. After reading this section, you may want to readjust your budget again to ensure that you are managing your finances the correct way. Remember, keep your pen handy and take notes!

Cash Flow Problem

One of the top reasons why your budget may not be working is because of actual income. Income is what funds our expenses, so without an adequate amount of income, it would be hard to pay for the things we want and need.

In order to budget correctly, you shouldn't live beyond your means. Some individuals are on a more restricted income and therefore must live as such. Others have multiple streams of income which allows them more buying power. Someone living strictly on social security or disability benefits may not be able to live in the same house or have the same expenses as someone who works full-time, or someone who has multiple streams of income. In order to gain financial stability, you must live based on what your income supplies.

You should always have an objective to earn as much income as possible, especially if you are trying to become financially successful. The good thing about our society today is that there are so many ways to generate more income. Passive income (making money in your sleep) is at an all-time high right now.

People are literally turning hobbies into cash. Take advantage of the opportunities that are available to you. Below are a few ways to earn additional income for you and your family that you might want to consider.

- Work overtime
- Overnight stock associate
- Complete online surveys
- Affiliate marketing
- Social media influencer
- Deliver groceries or fast food
- Get a temporary night job offered by temp agencies
- Work-from home data entry clerk or technical specialist
- Offer printing services (sell t-shirts, business cards, etc.)
- Tax preparer
- Virtual assistant
- Caterer
- Rent out rooms in your home or apartment
- Uber or Lyft driver
- Travel agent
- Sell old merchandise online or have a garage sale
- Photographer
- Create/sell an online course, seminar, or webinar
- Use personal talents to start a side business
- Make videos on platforms such as YouTube
- Custodian/ complete janitorial services at night
- Tutor/online teacher
- Baby or dog sitter/Pet-watcher
- Freelance writer or blogger
- Author-sell books or eBooks
- Mystery shopper
- Create an e-commerce business
- Write resumes and/or cover letters
- Investments (dividend income, rental income, etc.) As you begin to develop better and healthy relationships with money, your ultimate financial goal should be to invest. This generates the most income and is the most effective way to becoming financially successful.

Minimize Expenses

People tend to increase debt as their income increases which also results in a failed budget. We are more prone to buy more expensive cars and bigger houses just because there is an increase in income. In the financial world, this is known as lifestyle creep. Adding on more expenses is not the key to achieving financial success. It only leads to a decrease in personal net worth and more financial stress.

One of the most stated sayings I have heard is "I work hard, I should be able to buy what I want." Although this saying is true, you want to work hard so that you can enjoy the fruits of your labor. You work hard so that you can build generational wealth, retire at an early age, and live a joyful life without worrying about financial struggles. You don't want to be one of the ones driving around in a 2021 car just so you can show off while the monthly payments are becoming difficult to make. You don't want to work hard just so you can live in a big house and not be able to do anything because your mortgage is more than 28% of your income. You don't want to always be in debt.

You should always keep expenses as low as possible, even if your income increases. For example, when life was going great for me, I never thought about getting a new car at the time. My car was 15 years old, had dents in it, and chipped paint. At that time, I made enough to be able to get a new car, but I didn't. I enjoyed the ability to save and I'm glad I did because I needed that money later.

To ensure your expenses are as low as possible, consider these options:

- **Consider the Financial Rules of Thumb**

  Refer to the financial rules of thumb section to make sure your expenses are aligned to each percentage. Remember, your car note should be no more than 15% of your monthly take home pay. Follow the 28/36 or 50/30/20 rule. Keep retirement in the forefront of your thoughts!

- **Eliminate Any Unused Monthly Subscriptions**

  Do you have a gym membership that you don't use? Do you really read the magazine subscriptions you signed up for? When is the last time you watched something on Hulu? You could be savings hundreds of dollars by eliminating these expenses.

- **Create a Food, Gas, and Personal Spending Budget**

  You literally could be "eating" or "wearing" your financial freedom because of poor spending habits. Set a personal spending limit and stick to it. For those that have difficulty in eliminating personal spending, consider the 7-day rule. This is a great way to handle impulse buying. The 7-day rule states that if you want something (new outfit, shoes, etc.) wait 7 days and if you still want it, see if your budget will allow you to purchase it. The objective here is to change your mind about purchasing that particular item.

- **Switch to a More Affordable Phone or Insurance Company**

  With so many telephone and insurance companies available, you have the flexibility of choosing a company that will offer the lowest rates with the best benefits. Their objective is to offer the best deal, with hopes of you becoming a valuable member.

As a bonus, sometimes companies offer bundle deals and cut costs on services to appear more affordable compared to its competitors. Two years ago, for example, I switched phone companies and now my bill is $35 cheaper with better service per month. This one bill alone has allowed me to save $420 a year. In addition, they also offer cable, security, and internet packages that helped me to save more money too.

Insurance bundle deals work the same way. Bundling your home and auto insurance provides added discounts. You can also get discounts for things such as having a security system in your home or get a discount if you are retired.

Raising the deductible on your insurance can also help to cut cost. Just make sure the deductible is not too high that causes you to not be able to pay if in fact there is an incident.

- ## Refinance your Home or Car

  Before using this strategy, weigh the pros and cons. If your interest rate is extremely high and you're in a better financial situation now, I would suggest to refinance.

  Many individuals believe the objective is to lower monthly costs, which is true, but it's really to minimize the amount of interest on the overall loan. For example, it won't be wise to refinance a car that only has 36 monthly payments left to a new loan of 48 months just because the payments are lower. With this scenario, you will spend more in interest over the life of the loan, which defeats the purpose.

  You can trade in your car but make sure there is more equity in the car so that you will be able to save. Make sure the new car is a great trade off. It should be less expensive and less costly for minor maintenance and repairs. You should refrain from trading in your relatively new car for an old car that will cost you more for repairs. That is not a good trade off. The trade should make sense.

  Remember, refinancing is mostly about lowering interest rates. You should also consider this method for other financial products such as credit cards too. This will help to lower the interest charged on purchases. Be mindful that this process does involve checking your credit. The higher the credit score, the lower the interest rate.

- ## Lower/Eliminate Cable TV Service

  Reducing or eliminating cable tv service is probably one of the first things you should do when lowering expenses. As account holders, we never try to find ways to reduce our monthly bill. We never take advantage of the many "hidden" discounts they have to offer.

Take the time to look at your current plan. We are so use to paying bills without realizing what we are actually paying for. While educating one of my clients, I was able to save her $60.00 a month ($720 a year), by calling the cable company and asking the representative for available discounts that she could take advantage of. The point was to get the best deal, which she did. She didn't have to change her plan or anything. They simply gave her a "loyalty" discount for being a customer for over 10 years. If she can do it, you can too. Imagine if my client had minimized the number of channels, she would have saved even more!

An alternative to cable would be to subscribe to services such as Hulu, Netflix, or purchase a Firestick to save more money on a monthly basis. Consider cutting cable and using one of those services.

- **Lower Utility Bills**

    When I was younger, my mother would tell me to cut the light off when I wasn't using it or wait until I had a full load to wash clothes. I used to think that she was nagging me. It wasn't until I started paying my own bills when I truly understood what she meant by those statements. Nowadays, I get upset with myself for leaving a light on or not adjusting the temperature before I head out to work. Yes, sometimes I catch myself acting like Julius from Everybody Hates Chris!

    Every little thing helps, from adjusting the temperature to the recommended company's utility settings, minimizing water usage, or using energy efficiency light bulbs. Avoid running the water before getting in the shower. Put the television on power saving mode if you tend to fall asleep with the television on. Try this for a month and you will see a difference in your monthly utility bill.

- **Learn to Use Coupons for Household Products and Groceries**

    I remember standing behind a lady at the grocery store one day, and I watched her total go from $36.00 to about $10.00. I was amazed and wondered, "How did she do that?" For that moment on, I figured out how to coupon. Couponing can save you hundreds of dollars over time. Even if you're not an extreme coupon user, saving $2.00 on detergent or $3.00 on toothpaste can add up to big savings. There are several ways you can learn to coupon. Personally, I learned by watching several YouTube videos, visiting social media sites, and by trial and error.

    There are many ways you can get coupons. If you know someone that gets the Sunday newspaper, ask for their coupon section. You can print free coupons online or visit your local library and get some for free as well. Look at the weekly ads, there are always discounts available, especially with a membership. Get the app and download digital coupons. This is the easiest way to get coupons. It only takes a few clicks to become available to use. To get the best deal with couponing, look for deals that offer coupons and discounts on the same product. Double whammy!

- ## Don't Try to Keep Up with the Joneses

  Who are the Joneses anyway? What does their financial health look like? Are they truly financially stable?

  Social media can cause us to idolize false well-beings. It's almost like we praise debt. We get caught up in trying to compete with the "Joneses" that we neglect our own financial situations. People would rather take out a $30,000.00 car loan while only making $35,000.00 a year, just to be socially accepted. The bigger the house, the more "likes on social media".

  Don't try to compare your life to someone else. You don't know how they are making monthly payments. In fact, they could be struggling just to make ends meet. Focus on you and your own finances. So what if your friend just got a new house? So what if your next-door neighbor just purchased a new car? You are doing better than them already by just reading this book. Focus on achieving your financial goals and one day you'll be able to get a new house and car of your dreams, the right way.

Developing Healthy Financial Habits

Budgets fail because of bad financial habits. Take a moment to think about any bad habits you have when it comes to finances. Could it be that you are buying too much clothing? Gambling? Eating out too much? Whatever it is, write it down below.

_____

_____

_____

_____

_____

_____

_____

_____

_____

_____

_____

_____

_____

_____

_____

_____

_____

_____

_____

_____

_____

_____

_____

_____

_____

_____

_____

Now that you have it written down, it's time to take action and change it. The key to changing a behavior is to first admit that there is an issue, then create strategies to change the behavior.

So, what are your bad habits?

Is it eating out too much? Why do you eat out too much? Is it because of the taste? If so, Pinterest has an assortment of copy-cat recipes that you can use to cook the same meals at home.

Do you enjoy the experience of being in a restaurant? If so, set up your table in your own home to resemble a restaurants setting. Don't have time to cook? Try preparing your meals in advance. Take a day out of the week and cook/ prep your meals for the week.

For me, the biggest issue was purchasing items from the Amazon website. With just a click of a button, I could get just about anything I needed or wanted. I noticed that there were so many things I really didn't need, and to make matters worse, I had my credit card attached to the account. I didn't know the effects of my bad behavior until I began my financial journey on eliminating debt. Don't get me wrong, I still shop on Amazon, but I only get what I need, and I make sure it is a part of my personal spending budget. Understanding bad behaviors prevents overspending. Take the time to figure out what behaviors are causing you to miss out on achieving your financial goals. A list of tips and strategies to help with personal spending habits is provided later in chapters 9 and 10.

Not Including All Expenses

As stated previously, many individuals only budget for things such as car and house payments but neglect to create a budget for food, gas, and personal spending. In order to create an effective budget, you must include EVERY expenditure for the month.

While some expenses may not occur monthly, they can occur yearly. Expenses such as car taxes, school expenses, and anniversaries, are just a few of these expenses. To stay on track with your budget, I recommend creating a yearly expense worksheet. List all yearly expenses by due date. When it's time to create your next monthly budget, refer to the yearly expense worksheet and incorporate the expense into your budget. By doing so, you can avoid withdrawing from your savings account or using credit cards unnecessarily.

Buying in Bulk versus Making Small Purchases

Are you someone that buys coffee every morning before work at Starbucks? Do you make small purchases at convenience stores? Do you eat out for breakfast, lunch, and/or dinner every day?

These purchases may seem small, but if you were to add each small purchase, you would realize that it is better to buy in bulk. If you were to go to a convenience store every day for a week and buy a bag of chips and soda, it will cost you about $3.00. For the week, that will total $21.00. If you were to buy a bigger bag of chips and soda at the grocery store, it will cost only about $10.00. Just in that week alone, you will have saved $11.00. If you were to continue this for a year, you will have an additional savings of $572.00! This money could be used to pay for any unexpected car repairs or bills. You can also add it to your emergency savings fund. Can you imagine how much savings you would have if you did this for every small purchase you've made? What if you packed your lunch versus spending $10.00 every day? What if you shopped at Sam's Club, a bulk wholesale market, versus putting $2.00 a day in the vending machine? Over a year's time, you could be saving thousands of dollars. Limit small purchases and consider buying in bulk. You will end up saving more than you realize.

Miscalculations

Miscalculations can also lead to a failed budget. Sometimes we may underestimate just to make our budget work on paper, but in reality, it doesn't work. Can you really spend only $100 a month for a family of three on groceries? Is your electricity bill still only going to be $50.00 a month when you had your AC set to 68 degrees all summer?

When calculating expenses, always remember to round up or overestimate. If you average about $100.00 - $150.00 per week in groceries, round the total up to $150.00. If your car insurance is $126.00, round the total to $130.00 for the month. By doing this, you gain flexibility in your account to save or add more towards a financial goal. Don't set yourself up for failure. Remember to be realistic.

This rule should not only apply to expenses, but for income too. As stated previously, never include anticipated income. For hourly employees, figure out how many hours you've worked for the week and base your income from previous weeks. For individuals with fluctuated income, remember to perform a trend analysis.

Trying to Accomplish too Many Financial Goals at Once

There are times when eagerness is overpowering, clouding our financial goals. Things such as trying to save $1000.00 a month while trying to pay off high-interest rate credit cards, investing in 401(k)'s, IRA's, and other retirement accounts, all while trying to save for college. Focusing on all of these goals at one time becomes an added pressure due to insufficient income and may cause the budget process to fail.

As your income increases, it provides more opportunities to accomplish your financial goals. Try focusing on one goal at a time. More than likely, you are in the beginning stages of your financial growth process. Start off by saving $1000.00 - $2000.00 first. Once you have achieved this goal, begin focusing on eliminating debt. This helps to become more organized, which relieves stress, and helps to achieve goals that much quicker!

Using the Same Budget Every Month

Budgets tend to fail because the same strategy may not work every month. Calculations may not be the same month to month. Fixed expenses, (rent, car note, insurance, etc.) should be paid at the same time and are usually the same amount, but other expenses are generally not the same. If it's your turn to supply food for your child's football team, your food budget may increase for that month. It might be time for your car's quarterly oil change. First time mommy? Your living expenses will not be the same anymore.

Make your budget work for you. Personally, for me, I save more in the beginning of the year because towards the end of the year I have to worry about hurricane season, car maintenance, household expenses I purchase in bulk to last for the year, and any holiday expenses. Since I know this, my "savings budget" is much higher in the beginning of the year compared to the end of the year. I know that I must be very aggressive at the beginning of the year to achieve my financial goals by year end.

It is perfectly okay to adjust your budget from time to time. This means that you are aware of your current circumstances. This statement, however, does not suggest buying the newest iPhone or shoes to avoid putting money into your savings account. It could mean increasing your savings amount by $50 because your electricity bill was $50 less this month. It could mean using funds that was intended to be put into your emergency fund to make an extra credit card payment instead.

Also, be sure to avoid the phrase "I'll pay it next month". Next month becomes the next month until eventually you have to dig into your savings account or swipe your credit card to handle the financial obligation. If you know a bill has to be paid, make the necessary adjustments to your monthly budget. Don't forget to create your yearly expense worksheet!

Having Only One Bank Account Versus Multiple Bank Accounts

Budgets tend to fail because bank accounts are not organized based on the variety of transactions that occur. Since we have so many financial obligations, it's imperative to separate expenses as such. In order to organize your finances better, it is recommended to have three bank accounts. The first account should be for household bills. This account should be used strictly for bills, food, and gas. The second account should be your savings account. The last account should be your personal/miscellaneous spending account. This strategy works with the 50/30/20 financial rule of thumb. When your direct deposit is transacted, 50% of your paycheck should be deposited into the bill account, 30% should be deposited into the miscellaneous/personal account and the remaining 20% should be split into the savings and retirement accounts.

ALL OF THE ACCOUNTS SHOULD BE FREE! If you are subject to fees because of opening an additional account, consider another financial institution.

As you become more disciplined, I recommend having more than three bank accounts. A sample strategy is shown below.

Checking account #1-Bill account

Checking account #2-Food and gas account

Checking account #3-Personal spending account

Savings account #1-Regular Savings (Sinking fund/Money Challenge account-Will discuss later)

Savings account #2- Emergency Fund

Savings account(s) #3- Investment account (401(k), IRA, brokerage accounts, etc.)

This strategy may or may not work for you. Maybe you will only need three accounts. Maybe you need more than six. Either way, figure out a plan that works for you. You should always have more than one account to organize your finances.

Sinking Fund Expense Account

Sinking fund expenses can also cause a failed budget. Sinking funds are funds that are used to pay for expenses that typically "sink" (deplete) your bank account. Medical expenses, family emergencies, vacations, and car repairs, are just some examples. In a sense, these expenses automatically put you behind financially because they don't usually occur monthly and can sometimes pop up unexpectedly. Since this is true, you want to save properly so that you will be able to handle these expenses when they occur.

If you drive a relatively older car or if you have a child that periodically needs medical treatment, it would be wise to create a sinking fund account. This eliminates the feeling of "falling two steps behind" when the expense occurs.

The biggest misconception about an emergency fund is that it should cover your sinking expenses too. This is not accurate. If you use your emergency fund (3 - 6 months' worth of income) to pay for vacations, you are only robbing yourself if something happens to you drastically (lose a job, get a divorce, or experience a decrease in income). You should have a sinking fund account to pay for these expenses. Remember to keep regular savings and emergency fund accounts separate.

Believe You Can Achieve Financial Success

The last reason why budgets fail is because of the mindset that it won't work. If you continuously insert negative connotations, it only results in failure and self-sabotage. I like to think of this as the self-fulfilling prophecy. Speaking negativity eventually emanates from within and transfers into a reality.

How many times have you said to yourself, "My credit card balance is too high, I will never be able to pay it off" or "I will never be able to save $1000.00"? Negative thoughts equal negative results. Never doubt your ability to achieve financial success. It may take time and dedication but it's doable.

Never limit yourself. Set audacious goals. Instead of saying "I will never save $1000.00", try saying "I will become wealthy". Instead of complaining about high credit card balances say, "I will no longer have to use my credit card" or "I will become debt free". Speaking positivity only brings forth positivity. You just never know, an unexpected financial increase may occur to handle your financial responsibilities.

Now that you have an in-depth understand of budgeting, I want you to review your budget again. Think about the reasons why budgets fail and apply it to your situation. Are you miscalculating your expenses? Are there any ways you can generate more income? Have you changed your mindset about your financial situation and ready to set audacious goals?

It only gets better from here! Don't stop now! You are closer to achieving your goals than you think!

CHAPTER 4

HOW TO SAVE

I remember making a social media post about what issues people have when it comes to personal finance and the majority of the responses were not being able to save. Saving can be hard, especially when the unexpected happens. Like, driving to work and your tire blows or finding out your child need braces.

From my perspective and experience, there are two simple reasons why people have a hard time saving. The first reason is due to the lack of sufficient income and the second reason is because people don't prepare for the unexpected. Here are some simple questions to ask yourself: When you receive extra cash, do you spend it, or do you deposit it into your savings account? When you get paid, do you pay your bills first or take a vacation first, then worry about bills later? Are you living beyond your means?

Saving is very important because it allows you to prepare for the unexpected. It keeps you financially ahead. When you build a savings account, unexpected circumstances in your life should become a financial inconvenience and not a financial burden. When you find out that you need new tires for the car, you should be able to buy new tires without having to struggle significantly until you receive the next paycheck.

An important part of budgeting is saving. It is just as important as paying bills. In actuality, saving is more important than buying new clothes, shoes, and other wants. Saving money is a necessity!

Before you say, "I can't save" remember the self-fulfilling prophecy. If you say you can't then you won't. Take a moment to think about how you save. Write it down below.

_____

_____

_____

_____

Now that you have your strategy written down, I want to teach you some tips and strategies that has helped me to rebuild my savings. Is your pen out of ink yet? If so, grab another one because there is so much more to learn!

Ways to save:

- **Follow the 50/30/20 financial rule of thumb**

  Remember 20% of income should go towards savings (emergency fund, retirement accounts, etc.) And, if you want to achieve more financial success, change the percentage to 30% or higher. If you have difficulty with transferring funds, set your direct deposit to have 20% - 30% automatically going towards your saving goals. This helps to avoid the temptation of spending your savings.

- **Include a "savings expense" in your budget**

  Treat savings like a monthly bill too.

- **Separate your accounts/open a savings account**

  If you place all of your money in one account, more than likely you will spend more because there is more available to spend. Separating your accounts helps to avoid overspending. It helps to organize and prioritize your finances better. Create a separate savings account and remember to pay yourself first.

- **Save any unexpected earnings**
  Save that bonus check. Any compensation received for overtime pay should be saved too. When it comes to gaining financial stability, there is no such thing as extra money. Unexpected earnings should always be put towards a financial goal.

- **DO NOT withdraw from your savings for non-emergencies**

You received an email from one of your favorite online stores. The email states that the online store is offering 30% off but for today only. Ladies, your favorite dress is now on sale. Guys, your favorite shoes are also on sale. You check your budget and realize that you only have enough money for food and gas until next week when you get paid. Your personal spending budget has already reached its limit for the month.

What do you do?

_____
_____
_____

Sometimes we get caught up in the YOLO (you only live once) life ideology, that we forget about the future. Taking away from a savings account for non-emergencies is only hurting you in the end. Before withdrawing, consider the following questions to ask yourself:

1. Do I really need it?
2. Why do I need it?
3. Am I withdrawing the money to handle a financial inconvenience or withdrawing money to pay for a desired item that I want?
4. Can I wait until I have more personal spending money available to purchase this item?

I know you want to look nice for your friend's birthday party. I know that new restaurant just opened in your area, but is it a part of your budget? Is it helping you to become one step closer to achieving your financial goals? Poor personal spending habits hinders you from attaining financial freedom, so DON'T DO IT!

This also applies to retirement savings accounts too

- **Increase income**

  As mentioned previously, income is what funds our expenses. Without an adequate amount of income, it would be hard to accomplish what we need to do.

  Sometimes it can become difficult to save because we barely have money for food and gas. This is where you would need to reevaluate your living conditions. Are you spending too much in rent? Are bad personal spending habits taking the majority of your paycheck? What about food? Do you take advantage of coupons, buy 1 and get 1 free sales? Are you shopping at expensive grocery stores?

In addition to this, you should think about ways to increase personal cash flow. Refer back to Chapter 3 on ways to generate additional cash flow. Choose 2 or 3 options and begin to increase your income. People are literally turning hobbies and passions into profits and so can you!

If you only have one source of income now, think about how you can increase it. Go for that promotion. If you have a business, start a new product line. Collaborate with someone to increase profits. Have you seen a millionaire with only one source of income?

The more income you generate, the more you have to save and achieve your financial goals.

- **Minimize expenses**

We tend to think that increasing income is the only way to save. The less you have going out, the more you have available to save and achieve other financial goals. Remember, PAY YOURSELF FIRST. Don't think about giving your cable company $100.00 a month (which equals $1200.00 yearly) if you don't have $1200.00 in a savings account already. Never let expenses weigh your financial progress down.

- **Write a list before you shop**

Call me old-fashioned, but I just have to take my grocery list with me when I go shopping. This includes going to Wal-Mart or Target too. Sometimes we can get distracted on things we think we need and end up spending more than we should. How many of you went to Target for a shirt and ended up with shoes, electronics, and household items that you do not necessarily need? And what about grocery shopping? How many of you have set yourself up by shopping on an empty stomach?

Writing a list helps to avoid the temptation of overspending. If you want to be more proactive, check the prices beforehand so there won't be any surprises at checkout. Compare prices and brand labels. You can save more by choosing generic brand items. For those of you with a relatively large family, shop for food items that you can eat more than once. Spaghetti and Alfredo go a long way! Again, take advantage of weekly specials and check for digital and in-store coupons.

- **Meal-prep to save on food expenses**

Meal preparation saves time and money. Sometimes we get busy and are tired from working all day that we rarely have time to cook breakfast, lunch, or dinner. For us, it is very convenient to just "grab n go." Unfortunately, the amount of money spent on eating out becomes much higher compared to grocery shopping in the long run.

Instead of grabbing a meal on the go, try preparing your meals in advance. I have learned over the years that this method does work. Having sometimes worked 2 jobs and going to school was quite hectic. Adding a third job in the mix made it even more complicated. Because of a hectic schedule, I used one day of the week (Sunday) to grocery shop and prep meals for the week. With this method, I spent between $50.00 - $70.00 for the week (Monday-Friday) on groceries for breakfast, lunch, dinner, and snacks. Had I chosen the "grab n go" method, my food expense would increase to about $75-$150 for the week (assuming each meal is priced between $5 and $10). By using this method, I eliminated approximately $100-$200 in food expenses each month.

Let's not forget about how preparing your meals in advance helps save time too. It eliminates constant trips to the grocery store (saves money on gas), dinner can be cooked or ready earlier, and the cleanup process during the week is quicker too. It provides more time to sit with your children after work and help them with homework and it creates more time for extracurricular activities without having to rush home to cook dinner every day.

Figure out a strategy that works best for you. Are you off on Tuesdays? Instead of using it to do nothing, try meal-prepping or shopping for discounts. Do you work nights? Try cooking your meals in the morning so that you will have food for later. Get in the habit of eating leftovers too. Buy items in bulk. Before going through a drive-thru, think about what you have at home. Would you rather eat out to satisfy a craving, or get a stomach full with what you have at home so you can be one step closer to achieving your financial goals? The choice is yours, so choose wisely.

- **Bargain shop**

   Have you seen the news lately? So many big name brand stores are going bankrupt. Why is that?

   In recent years, there has been a change in consumer shopping. Consumers are becoming more frugal in everyday shopping and you should too. Instead of paying for the name brand item, consumers are shopping at discounted department stores such as Ross, TJ Maxx, local consignment shops, and thrift stores. Some of these stores offer high quality merchandise for almost half the price.

   Bargain shopping is a great way to save. You will be surprised by what you can find discounted. Be careful when shopping for discounts. With the variety of merchandise available, it could cause you to unintentionally overspend. Always set a limit.

   Not only should you bargain shop for everyday merchandise, you should do it for every financial decision you make too. Compare car insurance rates. Think about which car is going to cost the least overall. Which college is more affordable? Bargain shopping wins all the time!

- **Take advantage of free-99 and discounts!**

   Prior to my own financial journey, I used to get upset with people in the line who wanted a discount, regardless of how minimal the discount was. Today, I am that person. I see the value in finding discounts and I want to save money just like everyone else.

When you think about saving, it's important to always take advantage of the words free and discount. Sometimes we get caught up in always paying the face value, that we never take advantage of deals that could help us to save money.

Take the scenario I talked about earlier with the lady who total went from $36.00 down to about $10.00. Throughout most of my life, especially during my college days, when I considered myself to be broke, I was spending between $5.00 - $10.00 on detergent, toilet paper, and toothpaste, when I could've paid a lot less for those items. I'm pretty sure I gave away thousands of free dollars.

Remember to take advantage of rewards points, cash back rewards, digital coupons, and in store deals. Check your email for other rewards. You just might have something free waiting for you, especially if it's your birthday. Save your receipts too! You can earn cash and rewards for uploading receipts on apps such as Receipt Hog, Ibotta, Fetch rewards, and let's not forget about Retail Me Not. *I just love that website*, there are always discounts available for a variety of stores.

Along with merchandising, take advantage of free events in your community too. Use social media to find free or discounted webinars and seminars. Eventbrite, an event management service, is a great application to have on your phone if you are looking for local events. In using this app, I have been able to attend several free financial workshops to increase my knowledge. If you have children, take advantage of free kid-friendly events, restaurants with "kids eat free" nights, or visit the local park for some good old-fashioned fun.

Think of your favorite hobby. How can you make it free or discounted? Are you taking advantage of your loyalty points? Don't just let the points expire. It never hurts to ask for a military, student, or senior citizen discount wherever you go too.

- **Learn to say NO!**

I had to learn how to say no! There were times when people would ask to borrow money because of their careless financial decisions or because they knew I would always say yes without hesitation. I always felt like I had the letters "ATM" written on my forehead.

For a while, I carried the weight of others financial burden, but I had to realize that I couldn't keep doing that because I was only hurting myself financially. How could I get ahead if I was continuously bound by other's bad financial decisions?

I understand that people can truly be in a financial bind from unforeseen life situations. Life does happen, but when it gets to the point that you enable bad financial behaviors, it needs to stop. It is important for you to learn to say no, to ensure your own financial stability.

It is very easy for others to try to make you feel bad for saying no to them but, it is necessary. No matter if you get called selfish and have other negative influences that try to persuade you to say yes, DO NOT give in. You don't have to feel guilty about protecting your financial well-being. This is NOT an act of selfishness. You can't save money if you continuously give to those who do not try to save or fail to care about their financial well-being.

- **Save loose change.**

Find an old jar at home and start placing your change in there after each purchase. You will be surprised at how much you save over time.

- **Small savings = BIG savings!**

How many times in your life have you said, "It's just $10.00 dollars?" Just think about it.

$10.00 doesn't really seem like a lot, but it actually is.

Imagine, for the past 10 years, instead of saying "It's just $10 dollars" you decided to put that $10.00 into a savings account every week.

10 years = 120 months = 521 weeks

521 weeks* $10.00 = $5,210.00!

That's an additional $5,210.00 you could have in your savings account by simply putting $10.00 away a week. (Not including interest)

Let's go further, what if you were to contribute this amount into an IRA, 401(k), or a brokerage account? With the anticipated higher rate of return, the ending value of $10 a week will be much greater than $5,210! Always save, no matter how small you think the amount is.

- **Do-it-yourself (DIY)**
Another way to save, is by simply doing things on your own. Using resources such as "YouTube" or "Pinterest" are great platforms to use to learn how to do your own hair and make-up. You can also learn how to repair various electronics and appliances.

Personal Share:

A few years ago, I wanted to give my entire family a Christmas gift, but being the frugal person that I am, I wanted an inexpensive way of doing it. I went to Dollar Tree and Wal-Mart to buy poster boards, picture frames, stickers, and glue. I printed out pictures I'd taken with my mobile phone. I created a family collage and the ending product was so cute. My family loved it and I spent less than $25.

Think about what you can do yourself. Guys, can you cut your own grass? Ladies, can you do your own manicure and pedicure? DIY may cost you time, but it definitely saves you money.

- ## Use your "winning seasons" to get ahead for any "drought seasons"

Sometimes life can go so well with us in terms of finances. New job, new promotion, two incomes, money in abundance flowing through. We get so happy about additional income when we're "winning" but forget about saving for a "rainy day".

A life changing event gave me a dose of reality. What if I decided to use my part-time checks on unnecessary things? What if I used my bonuses for nonsense? I never knew that I would experience a drought season, but I made sure to always save just in case.

Preparing for the unexpected is how to handle the unexpected. Never assume that you will always have income without having to deal with life situations. Unfortunately, there are some financial obligations that you must deal with, such as car repairs or replacing household appliances. During your winning season, use this time to get ahead financially.

- ## Participate in money challenges

Have you heard about money challenges?

Money challenges are another unique way to save money. They are designed to help you put money aside every day, week, or month, so by the end of the challenge, you'll be able to save a specific amount. Money challenges are easy and fun because it doesn't feel like the traditional savings method. Once the challenge is complete, you'll feel accomplished, which is a great feeling.

One of the most common and popular money challenges used for many years is the 52-week challenge. The challenge requires you to deposit $1.00 in week 1, $2.00 in week 2, $3.00 in week 3, so forth and so on. By week 52 you will end up with $1,378.00.

As the challenge goes on, it can become tricky towards the end. Assuming you start in January, it becomes very difficult because the largest deposits are due in October-December. During this time, funds are mostly limited because you have to pay for Thanksgiving, Christmas, and traveling costs to visit loved ones. You have to become more aggressive in saving because the amount to deposit becomes larger.

A solution to this problem that I have found very helpful is rearranging the challenge. During weeks when more money is available, simply deposit more money, and during weeks when there is less money available, deposit less. Below is an example:

January:

Week 1: Deposit $52

Week 2: Deposit $15

Week 3: Deposit $25

Week 4: Deposit $10

This is a great way to complete the challenge. Make sure you have a printed copy of the challenge to keep track. Scratch off each amount once it is deposited in your savings account. Open a separate savings account if you need to. Also, try to save the lower deposited amounts towards the end of the year to make it easier to complete the challenge.

There are many other challenges available that will help you to save. Below are a few helpful money challenges that you can use to help jumpstart better saving habits. (The 52-week challenge is included.)

$5 a dollar/60-day challenge: *Total saved=$300*

Day	Amount Deposited	Balance	Day	Amount Deposited	Balance
1	$ 5.00	$ 5.00	31	$ 5.00	$ 155.00
2	$ 5.00	$ 10.00	32	$ 5.00	$ 160.00
3	$ 5.00	$ 15.00	33	$ 5.00	$ 165.00
4	$ 5.00	$ 20.00	34	$ 5.00	$ 170.00
5	$ 5.00	$ 25.00	35	$ 5.00	$ 175.00
6	$ 5.00	$ 30.00	36	$ 5.00	$ 180.00
7	$ 5.00	$ 35.00	37	$ 5.00	$ 185.00
8	$ 5.00	$ 40.00	38	$ 5.00	$ 190.00
9	$ 5.00	$ 45.00	39	$ 5.00	$ 195.00
10	$ 5.00	$ 50.00	40	$ 5.00	$ 200.00
11	$ 5.00	$ 55.00	41	$ 5.00	$ 205.00
12	$ 5.00	$ 60.00	42	$ 5.00	$ 210.00
13	$ 5.00	$ 65.00	43	$ 5.00	$ 215.00
14	$ 5.00	$ 70.00	44	$ 5.00	$ 220.00
15	$ 5.00	$ 75.00	45	$ 5.00	$ 225.00
16	$ 5.00	$ 80.00	46	$ 5.00	$ 230.00
17	$ 5.00	$ 85.00	47	$ 5.00	$ 235.00
18	$ 5.00	$ 90.00	48	$ 5.00	$ 240.00
19	$ 5.00	$ 95.00	49	$ 5.00	$ 245.00
20	$ 5.00	$100.00	50	$ 5.00	$ 250.00
21	$ 5.00	$105.00	51	$ 5.00	$ 255.00
22	$ 5.00	$110.00	52	$ 5.00	$ 260.00
23	$ 5.00	$115.00	53	$ 5.00	$ 265.00
24	$ 5.00	$120.00	54	$ 5.00	$ 270.00
25	$ 5.00	$125.00	55	$ 5.00	$ 275.00
26	$ 5.00	$130.00	56	$ 5.00	$ 280.00
27	$ 5.00	$135.00	57	$ 5.00	$ 285.00
28	$ 5.00	$140.00	58	$ 5.00	$ 290.00
29	$ 5.00	$145.00	59	$ 5.00	$ 295.00
30	$ 5.00	$150.00	60	$ 5.00	$ 300.00

Deposit a different amount each day for 90 days: Total saved=$500

$ 1.00	$ 10.00	$ 1.00	$ 1.00	$ 1.00	$ 1.00	$ 1.00	$ 20.00	$ 1.00
$ 1.00	$ 1.00	$ 1.00	$ 5.00	$ 1.00	$ 5.00	$ 5.00	$ 5.00	$ 1.00
$ 5.00	$ 10.00	$ 5.00	$ 1.00	$ 5.00	$ 5.00	$ 5.00	$ 10.00	$ 5.00
$ 1.00	$ 5.00	$ 10.00	$ 10.00	$ 5.00	$ 1.00	$ 1.00	$ 20.00	$ 5.00
$ 1.00	$ 20.00	$ 5.00	$ 1.00	$ 10.00	$ 20.00	$ 1.00	$ 1.00	$ 1.00
$ 5.00	$ 1.00	$ 1.00	$ 5.00	$ 5.00	$ 5.00	$ 10.00	$ 5.00	$ 1.00
$ 20.00	$ 5.00	$ 1.00	$ 1.00	$ 5.00	$ 20.00	$ 5.00	$ 1.00	$ 1.00
$ 5.00	$ 5.00	$ 5.00	$ 1.00	$ 5.00	$ 10.00	$ 1.00	$ 5.00	$ 10.00
$ 20.00	$ 5.00	$ 10.00	$ 5.00	$ 20.00	$ 5.00	$ 5.00	$ 5.00	$ 1.00
$ 1.00	$ 10.00	$ 1.00	$ 10.00	$ 5.00	$ 1.00	$ 10.00	$ 1.00	$ 10.00

Deposit a different amount each day for 90 days: Total saved=$1000

$ 5.00	$ 10.00	$ 25.00	$ 5.00	$ 1.00	$ 10.00	$ 25.00	$ 20.00	$ 10.00
$ 1.00	$ 20.00	$ 30.00	$ 1.00	$ 15.00	$ 30.00	$ 15.00	$ 30.00	$ 1.00
$ 15.00	$ 25.00	$ 10.00	$ 1.00	$ 1.00	$ 5.00	$ 1.00	$ 10.00	$ 5.00
$ 1.00	$ 30.00	$ 20.00	$ 5.00	$ 15.00	$ 1.00	$ 1.00	$ 5.00	$ 1.00
$ 20.00	$ 10.00	$ 30.00	$ 15.00	$ 20.00	$ 5.00	$ 10.00	$ 1.00	$ 5.00
$ 5.00	$ 1.00	$ 1.00	$ 10.00	$ 5.00	$ 1.00	$ 5.00	$ 15.00	$ 15.00
$ 1.00	$ 15.00	$ 5.00	$ 5.00	$ 25.00	$ 5.00	$ 1.00	$ 5.00	$ 1.00
$ 30.00	$ 15.00	$ 20.00	$ 1.00	$ 20.00	$ 30.00	$ 30.00	$ 20.00	$ 40.00
$ 1.00	$ 5.00	$ 10.00	$ 5.00	$ 1.00	$ 1.00	$ 15.00	$ 5.00	$ 1.00
$ 10.00	$ 1.00	$ 20.00	$ 1.00	$ 30.00	$ 5.00	$ 25.00	$ 5.00	$ 10.00

52 Week Challenge-Save $1378 in a year

Week	Amount Deposited	Balance	Week	Amount Deposited	Balance
1	$ 1.00	$ 1.00	27	$ 27.00	$ 378.00
2	$ 2.00	$ 3.00	28	$ 28.00	$ 406.00
3	$ 3.00	$ 6.00	29	$ 29.00	$ 435.00
4	$ 4.00	$ 10.00	30	$ 30.00	$ 465.00
5	$ 5.00	$ 15.00	31	$ 31.00	$ 496.00
6	$ 6.00	$ 21.00	32	$ 32.00	$ 528.00
7	$ 7.00	$ 28.00	33	$ 33.00	$ 561.00
8	$ 8.00	$ 36.00	34	$ 34.00	$ 595.00
9	$ 9.00	$ 45.00	35	$ 35.00	$ 630.00
10	$ 10.00	$ 55.00	36	$ 36.00	$ 666.00
11	$ 11.00	$ 66.00	37	$ 37.00	$ 703.00
12	$ 12.00	$ 78.00	38	$ 38.00	$ 741.00
13	$ 13.00	$ 91.00	39	$ 39.00	$ 780.00
14	$ 14.00	$ 105.00	40	$ 40.00	$ 820.00
15	$ 15.00	$ 120.00	41	$ 41.00	$ 861.00
16	$ 16.00	$ 136.00	42	$ 42.00	$ 903.00
17	$ 17.00	$ 153.00	43	$ 43.00	$ 946.00
18	$ 18.00	$ 171.00	44	$ 44.00	$ 990.00
19	$ 19.00	$ 190.00	45	$ 45.00	$ 1,035.00
20	$ 20.00	$ 210.00	46	$ 46.00	$ 1,081.00
21	$ 21.00	$ 231.00	47	$ 47.00	$ 1,128.00
22	$ 22.00	$ 253.00	48	$ 48.00	$ 1,176.00
23	$ 23.00	$ 276.00	49	$ 49.00	$ 1,225.00
24	$ 24.00	$ 300.00	50	$ 50.00	$ 1,275.00
25	$ 25.00	$ 325.00	51	$ 51.00	$ 1,326.00
26	$ 26.00	$ 351.00	52	$ 52.00	$ 1,378.00

10 Day- Did you pack your lunch challenge- Save $50

Day	Did you Pack Your Lunch Today?	Estimated Savings
1		$5
2		$10
3		$15
4		$20
5		$25
6		$30
7		$35
8		$40
9		$45
10		$50

12 Week Challenge-Save $1800

Week	Amount Deposited	Balance
1	$ 100.00	$ 100.00
2	$ 150.00	$ 250.00
3	$ 200.00	$ 450.00
4	$ 50.00	$ 500.00
5	$ 75.00	$ 575.00
6	$ 200.00	$ 775.00
7	$ 100.00	$ 875.00
8	$ 200.00	$1,075.00
9	$ 150.00	$1,225.00
10	$ 200.00	$1,425.00
11	$ 300.00	$1,725.00
12	$ 75.00	$1,800.00

Build Your First Emergency Fund Challenge- Save $1000

Month	Amount Deposited	Balance
1	$ 83.33	$ 83.33
2	$ 83.33	$ 166.66
3	$ 83.33	$ 249.99
4	$ 83.33	$ 333.32
5	$ 83.33	$ 416.65
6	$ 83.33	$ 499.98
7	$ 83.33	$ 583.31
8	$ 83.33	$ 666.64
9	$ 83.33	$ 749.97
10	$ 83.33	$ 833.30
11	$ 83.33	$ 916.63
12	$ 83.37	$1,000.00

Build Your First Emergency Fund Challenge- Save $2000

Month	Amount Deposited	Balance
1	$ 166.67	$ 166.67
2	$ 166.67	$ 333.34
3	$ 166.67	$ 500.01
4	$ 166.67	$ 666.68
5	$ 166.67	$ 833.35
6	$ 166.67	$1,000.02
7	$ 166.67	$1,166.69
8	$ 166.67	$1,333.36
9	$ 166.67	$1,500.03
10	$ 166.67	$1,666.70
11	$ 166.67	$1,833.37
12	$ 166.63	$2,000.00

Start your first sinking fund account challenge- Save $500

Month	Amount Deposited	Balance
1	$ 60.00	$ 60.00
2	$ 100.00	$ 160.00
3	$ 150.00	$ 310.00
4	$ 75.00	$ 385.00
5	$ 40.00	$ 425.00
6	$ 75.00	$ 500.00

Start your first sinking fund account challenge- Save $1000

Month	Amount Deposited	Balance
1	$ 75.00	$ 60.00
2	$ 300.00	$ 375.00
3	$ 100.00	$ 475.00
4	$ 150.00	$ 625.00
5	$ 125.00	$ 750.00
6	$ 250.00	$ 1,000.00

- **Breakdown your savings goals**

Do you know that simply saving $16.50 a day will allow you to have $6000 this time next year? That's the contribution limit for a Roth IRA (retirement account) in 2021.

Setting a specific savings goal may seem easy, but actually implementing the goal may become quite difficult. This is especially true if there is not a clear financial plan in place.

Personally, there were many years that I stated I would save $5,000 or $10,000 a year and fall short. A solution to this problem that I have found useful is to break the savings goal by day or week. Similar to the money challenges presented above, whenever you are finding it difficult to save, instead of trying to save large amounts each month, consider breaking down the amount by day or week.

Still uncertain that you can save? Try this strategy:

1. Save loose change: monthly savings - $10.00 = **$120.00 a year**

2. Cancel unused memberships: monthly savings - $20.00 = **$240.00 a year**

3. Switch car insurance: monthly savings - $30.00 = **$360.00 a year**

4. Switch phone/tablet plans to Wi-Fi only or no contract phones:

monthly savings - $40.00 = **$480.00 a year**

5. Lower cable bill-switch to Netflix and Hulu only: monthly savings - $50.00 = **$600.00 a year**

6. Learn to coupon monthly necessities: monthly savings- $50.00 = **$600.00 a year**

7. Buy groceries instead of eating out every day: monthly savings -$75.00 = **$900.00 a year**

TOTAL SAVINGS = $3,300.00!!!!!

You can do it. You just have to be willing to make the sacrifice!

CHAPTER 5

HOW TO ELIMINATE DEBT

This section contains a topic that everyone hates. Debt, debt, debt, blah, blah, blah. $12,000.00 in credit card debt, $20,000.00 car loan, $200,000.00 mortgage, and let's not forget the $120,000.00 in student loan debt. Debt can seem so overwhelming. It can make you feel so discouraged, especially if your debt amount increases every year.

There are many experts that can make you feel bad about being in debt. I remember watching a television series and the spokesperson made everyone hold up a sign to show how much debt they had. Pretty embarrassing right?

One of the biggest misconceptions is that all debt is bad debt. That is not true. Since most of us are not born into wealth, we must start somewhere. If you think about it, personal finance is not taught in school. Teachers/instructors don't teach you about loans, credit cards, and ways to generate income. It is traditionally taught by parents or learned from personal experience. Since many of our parents were never taught financial literacy, the pattern of not knowing about personal finance continues from generation to generation until someone breaks the cycle. When we are finally old enough to understand how to manage debt, it may be too late in terms of leveling debt.

More often than I'd like to admit, the reason why children are in debt is because their parents were in debt. Some have no choice but to accumulate student loan debt because their parents are not able to pay for education. Some have no choice but to get a loan because they have no capital to start a business from scratch. There is a chance that financial growth is possible without massive amounts of debt if children are taught from a young age about the different ways to make money, becoming an entrepreneur, and how to avoid debt. It is not impossible to become wealthy but, just don't expect it to come from an annual salary of $40,000.00 with a lot of bills to pay.

It's important to distinguish between good debt and bad debt. Debt should be used to build creditworthiness that in turn will allow for more opportunities to increase personal financial growth. Debt should not be used to fund daily activities. You shouldn't use debt (swipe your credit card) as a means of eating out or going shopping because you fail to budget. You shouldn't use debt to buy an expensive car that will ultimately cause you angst later.

When it comes to debt, the key to financial success is minimizing bad debt while focusing on using good debt to obtain better buying and negotiating power, gaining financial freedom, and entering entrepreneurship one day. When using good debt to your advantage, eventually you will become debt free.

In this section, I will provide ways to eliminate debt. In using the strategies below, ensure that you focus on eliminating bad debt (unnecessary credit card purchases, payday loans, etc.) first.

Ways to eliminate debt:

- **Increase income, follow the financial rules of thumb, and minimize expenses**

  I want to keep reintegrating this in your head. There are several opportunities available to increase your income. Minimizing expenses creates more opportunities for financial growth. The financial rules of thumb have been proven to help the individual accomplish financial success. Each rule helps to allocate your finances the correct way.

Refer to Chapter 3 on ways to generate additional income.

- Work overtime
- Overnight stock associate
- Complete online surveys
- Affiliate marketing
- Social media influencer
- Deliver groceries or fast food
- Get a temporary night job offered by temp agencies
- Work-from home data entry clerk or technical specialist
- Offer printing services (sell t-shirts, business cards, etc.)
- Tax preparer
- Virtual assistant
- Caterer
- Rent out rooms in your home or apartment
- Uber or Lyft driver
- Travel agent
- Sell old merchandise online or have a garage sale
- Photographer
- Create/sell an online course, seminar, or webinar
- Use personal talents to start a side business
- Make videos on platforms such as YouTube
- Custodian/complete janitorial services at night
- Tutor/online teacher
- Baby or dog sitter/Pet-watcher

- Freelance writer or blogger
- Author-sell books or eBooks
- Mystery shopper
- Create an e-commerce business
- Write resumes and/or cover letters

The items listed above are ways to generate income based on working or making a profit from products and services sold, but there are other ways to generate wealth. Multiple sources of income provides the most opportunities for financial growth. In order to succeed financially, you must earn money from more than one income source. Below are five other income streams to generate additional income:

1. **Interest income:** Income earned from interest rates. (ex. money earned from savings accounts, certificate of deposits (CD's), etc.)

2. **Rental income:** Income earned from rental property (ex. flipping houses, wholesaling, apartment rentals, etc.)

3. **Royalty income:** Income earned from intangible work or other intellectual property. (ex. trademarks, franchises, patents, etc.)

4. **Capital gain income:** Income earned due to investments being sold for a higher price compared to its original purchase price. (ex. financial speculator)

5. **Dividend income:** Income earned from the distribution of a company's earnings. When a company generates profits, as a shareholder (an individual who owes shares of stock), you will receive a portion of its earnings.

As you begin to develop better money habits, take advantage of having more than one source of income. Make it a goal to generate income from multiple sources.

- **Avoid adding on more bad debt**

  Having a budget is important to help avoid adding on more bad debt. As stated previously, we use debit cards until our bank accounts are fully depleted. Once this happens, then the credit cards are in heavy rotation, creating other bad debt, just to fund daily activities. The simplest way to get out of debt is to not use debt unnecessarily. Remember, the purpose of debt is to obtain better buying and negotiating power. Using debt correctly builds the foundation for positive financial growth.

- **Use any unexpected earnings to eliminate debt**

  Remember, there is no such thing as extra money. Any unexpected earnings should be used to achieve your financial goals quicker.

- **Focus on one goal at a time**

Simply paying $200.00, here, $300.00 there can sometimes become exhausting. It's also frustrating because the balances may never seem to go down. Focusing on one goal at a time makes the debt elimination process smoother and quicker. It can also become a motivator to tackle debt more aggressively and you can scratch it off your financial to do list.

One way to accomplish this is by handling your debts using the snowball method as mentioned previously. Start with the smallest debt. Make the highest payment you can make on the smallest debt while only paying the minimum payment on all of the other debts. Use the avalanche method if you have relatively high interest rates, which is to pay off debt according to the interest rate.

- **Consider debt consolidation**

Debt consolidation combines all of your debt into one loan to make it more simplified to handle all of your financial obligations. Debt consolidation is great, but understand the cons associated with it. There are two types of debt consolidation loans, secured and unsecured. Secured debt consolidation loans are relatively easy to get approved for, but it requires collateral. If you were to miss a payment, lenders can take your car or anything else you have as collateral. Unsecured debt consolidation doesn't require collateral, but it could be hard to get without a great credit score. The interest rate on unsecured debt consolidation loans tends to be higher. This is because lenders consider unsecured loans to be a little riskier. Debt consolidation is a preferred option for relatively large loans. Student loans are a great example. If you have student loans from several lenders, it would be best to consolidate your loans into one loan to help minimize the cost of high interest, make payments easier to manage, and make the loan more affordable for your budget.

- **Do a balance transfer - for credit cards**

Balance transfers are a great way to help minimize debt because it typically decreases the amount of interest to pay. A balance transfer is simply transferring the balance of one credit card to another credit card. Lenders typically offer a promotional interest rate of 0% for the first 6 – 18 months. Depending on the terms and conditions, you are not subject to paying interest for that particular time frame.

Balance transfers can be helpful in saving money due to interest rates as it combines all credit card debt onto one payment source. Be mindful that this only moves money from one card to another card. If you become irresponsible, more than likely you will use the credit card that you've transferred the balance from again. This only results in more debt. Consider balance transfers very carefully.

Should you consider a balance transfer, take advantage of the 0% interest rate. Look into any balance transfer fees and ensure the lender is a business entity that you'd want to build a credit relationship with. Develop a strategy that will allow you to pay your balance owed within the promotional period to save money on interest. This will help to minimize your credit card debt tremendously.

- **Complete a money challenge**

In addition to using a money challenge to save, you can also use it to pay off debt. Refer back to chapter 4.

- **Pay more than the minimum payment- (with the exception of the snowball method)**

Another way to eliminate debt is to pay more than the suggested payment. Minimum payments are designed to keep you in debt. The credit card company's mission, for example, is to make you pay as much interest as possible on the debt to profit more in return. This is evident in credit cards and other lines of credit. Review your credit card statement. If you notice, when the balance due becomes lower, the lender will lower the minimum payments with hopes that you will pay less. Why not keep the payments the same? You know why, don't be fooled!
To help reduce the overall cost on loans such as car loans and mortgages, consider making double payments. Once you make your first payment, apply the second payment to principle. This is known as a principle only payment. Principle only payments decreases principle, which decreases the amount of interest. Less principle=less interest. A principal only payment helps to not only save on interest but shortens the length of the loan as well. Before making principle only payments, read the terms of your loans. Not all loans allow this option and some lenders will charge you a fee.

- **For student loan debt**

Student loan debt is at an all-time high right now. Almost every individual that attends college ends up with student loan debt. The good thing is that you are reading this book so you can start preparing your children for college now! Below are a few tips to help minimize student loan debt.

1. Take out only want you need. Refund checks may seem like a good thing, but paying it back is not. A $3,000.00 refund check can turn into $5,000.00 or more over the life of the loan.
2. Choose in-state tuition versus out-of-state tuition.
3. Education tax credits (ex. The American Opportunity Tax Credit-AOTC)
4. Apply for scholarships, grants, and other tuition assistance programs.
5. Open a 529 college savings plan early.
6. Avoid forbearance. Just because you claim forbearance, remember, the interest still accrues.
7. Consider debt consolidation-don't just ignore your student loan debt.
8. Look for student loan forgiveness programs (ex. public service forgivingness, teacher loan forgivingness, etc.)
9. Try to lower college expenses
   - Rent books versus buy books (especially for classes that are not in your career field)
   - Work-study
   - Work part-time
   - Cook versus choosing an expensive meal plan
   - Carpool

- Attend a community college for general education classes then transfer to a 4-year college
- Seek employer-paid tuition programs
- Dual enrollment programs-take college classes in high school (make sure they are transferrable)
- Split living expenses with a roommate
- Military/Veteran assistance

10. Be mindful of the terms and conditions when it comes to repaying your student loans. Some student repayment loans are setup as negative amortization loans. Simply put, although you are making monthly payments, the outstanding balance on the loan will continue to increase every year. Make sure the monthly payment amount covers the cost of interest to avoid this.

- **Credit Counseling Agencies**
  If you are struggling with high debt, you can reach out to a local credit counseling agency. Counselors are available to help the debt elimination process smoother. They provide tips and strategies to help with financial issues related to bankruptcies, loan counseling, managing money, and other related financial topics. Credit counseling agencies sometimes offer free educational seminars and workshops as well.

CHAPTER 6

FINANCE FOR SINGLES

In your mind, do you believe that singleness is a good status or a bad status in regards to financial matters?

Many may feel that it is not a good thing to be single when it comes to finances. It's bad enough that you have to deal with all the responsibilities yourself, especially if you are a single parent. Daily living expenses can be very costly with only one income, making it a difficult task of making ends meet.

Although this is a fact, you must also know that there are couples surviving off of one income. More members in the household does not equate to more income in the household. Not everyone living in the house may be contributing financially. You may be doing better financially by yourself compared to a two-member household.

Embrace the season of singleness. This is the time to gain clarity and understand your financial health. Use this time to figure out your financial goals. You can work on fixing bad financial behaviors, increasing financial knowledge, and understand how you can contribute to your future relationship financially.

I may not be a relationship expert, but I can tell you that one of the top reasons why marriages fail is due to issues related to finance. So many people are ready to become one unit in matrimony, but fail to ensure they have a better understanding of their finances beforehand. Some neglect to talk about finances in general. As a single person, if you fail to budget, understand financial literacy, make smart financial decisions, or learn how to save now, it will become much harder to achieve financial success when you get into a relationship.

Here is what I mean:

It's human nature to increase debt once income increases. When one income becomes two, more than likely, household and other living expenses increase. The cable, electricity, and water consumption increases. Staying at home on a Saturday night has now turned into dinner at your favorite restaurant.

Credit card balances increase because of expensive birthday and anniversary gifts. Savings account balances decrease because eating hotdogs and spaghetti that once helped you to save each month has now turned into steak and potatoes, lobster, and pork chops every night. Bonuses received at work are now used to take vacations instead of making double payments on your car.
Need I say more?

It can be challenging to have to pay for everything on your own, but this phase only helps you to develop financial independence. If you are a single person, use this time to think about your personal financial goals. How are you handling your finances now? What do you want and expect in a relationship when it comes to finances? What financial goals do you want to achieve when you find your soulmate? Take a moment to write the answers down in the space below.

_____

_____

_____

_____

_____

_____

_____

_____

_____

_____

_____

_____

_____

_____

_____

_____

_____

_____

_____

_____

_____

Here are a few things that you can focus on now as a single person:

- Focus on budgeting to organize monthly income and expenses
- Work on improving your credit score
- Spend less, save more
- Create a debt elimination strategy
- Eliminate bad financial habits
- Turn your hobby into a business
- Think about ways to start saving for retirement
- Adjust living arrangements to minimize household expenses
- Work more if you have time
- Read more about personal finance
- Learn to cook less expensive meals now to save on your grocery bill in the future
- Create a list of goals you want and expect in your next relationship in terms of finances

Depending on your situation, it's okay to be the only person that provides the household income. Don't wait until someone else comes along to focus on achieving financial success. You have the ability to do this on your own as well. If you follow the 7 steps to creating your budget and stick to it, you will see financial growth in no time.

CHAPTER 7

FINANCE FOR COUPLES & CHILDREN

Did you pay the light bill this month?

I thought it was your turn to handle the groceries this week?

Can I borrow $40.00 until next week?

Does this sound familiar?

I'm no relationship expert, but I have personally seen and experienced how couples behave when it comes to finances. Too often, couples tend to handle their finances separately when it should be handled together. Since you are equally yoke, this means that your finances should become one. Most of the time, you have to file taxes together and what was once a tax refund is now a tax repayment. Income-based student loan payments that were once $200.00 has now doubled. Living expenses are the same too. This is why it is imperative to understand each other's financial health before saying I do.

Before doing anything else, if you haven't already, I want you to take this time and share with your spouse EVERYTHING that is going on with you financially. How much income are you currently making? Create a list of debt(s) that you both have. What financial goals are you trying to achieve together? What do you find that is working with your relationship in terms of finances? What is not working? Write this information in the space provided below.

_____

_____

_____

_____

_____

_____

_____

_____

_____

_____

_____

_____

_____

_____

_____

_____

_____

_____

_____

_____

_____

_____

_____

_____

_____

_____

Once you've understood where you are currently, identify what you want to accomplish together. Revisit the 7 steps to creating a budget section. Identify the combined household income. Create a household expense chart. Identify which expenses can be removed, canceled, or cut down. Work on paying off debts based on the lowest balances between you as a couple.

Not every couple will have the same budget. As stated previously, not every member in the household contributes financially. Not all wages are the same. Create a strategy for expenses so that it doesn't cause financial stress on the partner that makes less. Ensure all living conditions are not based solely on the person that makes the most. Each person should be allotted the same amount of personal spending each month.

To help simplify budgeting for families with more than one income, I recommend having 5 separate checking accounts.

Checking account #1: **Bill account-** The account should be used to handle all bills
Checking account #2: **Family account-**The account should be used for food, gas, and other family expenses
Checking Account #3: **Family Personal Spending Account-**The account can be used for shared dining and entertainment costs.

Checking Account #4: **Her Account-**The account should be used for her personal spending

Checking Account #5: **His Account-** The account should be used for his personal spending

This strategy helps to avoid the phrases of "Did you pay the light bill this month?" or "I thought it was your turn to handle the groceries this week?" It separates expenses to make things more simplified and equal, especially when it comes to personal spending.

In addition to monthly expenses, there should also be a strategy for saving. Figure out if you want to have a combined emergency fund or a separate emergency fund. Create a personal savings account for any unexpected personal expenses. Determine how much each of you will contribute to your 401(k)s and other retirement accounts. Create a family vacation savings account to avoid having one person pay more than the other.

Below is a helpful savings strategy:
Savings account(s) #1: **Regular family savings-** The account(s) should be used for unexpected family situations (can also be used to save for family vacations as well)

Savings account(s) #2: **Children savings-** The account(s) should be used to build generational wealth for children (can also be an investment account or another account offering a higher rate of return)

Savings account(s) #3: **Family investment fund -**The account(s) should be used to build personal net worth together.

Savings account(s) #4: **His account-** The account(s) is used for his personal savings (personal, retirement, investment, etc.)

Savings account(s) #5: **Her account-** The account(s) is used for her personal savings (personal, retirement, investment, etc.)

Couples should have one common goal. That goal should be to focus on building financial stability for their offspring and future heirs, opposed to financial illiteracy. Breaking generational curses and leaving a legacy of wealth is by far more pleasurable than passing down the lack of financial knowledge.
As your children grow, personal finance should be a part of their education. I know the lack of financial literacy stemmed from decades ago, but things are different today. Technical software such as the famous worldwide web (www) and social media platforms can be used to increase financial awareness. There is more opportunity now to learn about finance than it has ever been. Financial literacy is not

always taught in the school system, so it's up to parents to make sure children understand it. It's up to parents to make sure their children don't fall into the same bad patterns that they did. Enough of "not knowing". The change should begin NOW.

Personal History

There were so many things that I personally didn't know about finance until I had to experience it on my own. I wish I knew about it before. For example, when I was 19, I opened my first bank account by myself. I only went because the bank was giving away $25.00 instantly just for opening an account. I felt like an adult leaving the bank with my new checking and savings account. It wasn't until weeks later when I opened the mail and discovered a white card with paper wrapped around it. In my mind, I thought, *What is this? I already got a debit card, maybe it's just an ATM card.*

I remember calling my mother at work and boy was she confused and furious. "What did you do at that bank?" That was the first thing she said to me when I told her about the mail. Of course, not knowing everything, I stated, "I just opened a checking and savings account." She asked me to describe the card. The only thing I could say was it was a Visa with numbers and an expiration date. She ended up telling me that it was actually a credit card, she described what a credit card was, and told me to use it for emergency purposes only. That was my first and only lesson about credit cards at the time.

At the age of 20, and being a college student, anything and everything was considered an emergency to me. Situations like going to Wendy's at 11 p.m. was an emergency because I didn't want to eat ramen noodles again. I took trips to Charlotte, North Carolina and Atlanta, Georgia all on credit. Instead of using it for emergency purposes like my mother told me, I used it for nonsense. What made matters worse was that the bank kept increasing my credit limit despite not paying down the balance. The more they gave, the more I used. What quickly started as a credit limit of only $500.00, grew to a credit limit of $3,000.00, and was still steadily increasing as I swiped. With such ease, I maxed out the limit on my credit card in two years.

When I logged into creditkarma.com, I noticed my credit score drop from a 750 down to a 620. It took several years to pay off the balance because I wasn't working, and I was only making the minimum payments of $45.00, which $25.00 of the payment was applied to interest.

This story represents one reason why it is important to understand finance and teach your children about the importance of making smart financial decisions. At the age of 19, I never knew what a credit card was. I didn't know that my interest rate of 22.99 % was awful and one of the reasons why it was taking me so long to pay off the balance. I didn't know that my credit score would decrease again because I closed the card once I paid it off!

It's never too early to teach children about money and finance. I believe that the ripe ages of 6 to 8 years of age are an opportune time to teach them how money is earned. One way to allow children to get an understanding and develop a positive relationship with money is to allow them to perform chores around the house and earn money for the work they complete. Another means is to buy a piggy bank and show them the importance of saving. At the ages of 9 to 11, they should be taught how to bargain shop and learn how to become frugal. A trip to the grocery store can teach them how to compare prices and learn about discounts and free offers. Between the ages of 12 and 14, teach them about bank terminology, bills, and other expenses. Show them what a debit card looks like and how money is deducted from a checking account. When they enter high school, teach them about budgeting. Present them with real-life issues. Teach them about investments and ways to generate more income, other than the traditional method of working a job. Teach them about finding purpose and entrepreneurship. Find workshops and seminars that are free to help them understand personal finance better. Above all, make it a fun experience! Finance can seem boring, but there are games such as Monopoly and Life, to make it enjoyable.

I also have a financial activity workbook that is available on my website www.aliciasfinancialcorner.com ,which can teach them about personal finance. Create a weekly or monthly challenge, something like "how many chores can you do" challenge. These challenges and activities will not only teach them about money, but it helps keep the house clean too. Remember, education is the key to financial success! Instead of giving your child what you never had, teach them what you never knew.

CHAPTER 8

THE WORLD OF BANKING

Have you ever visited a bank and the banker was seemingly speaking another language to you like suggesting how beneficial it would be to apply for a credit card because your account was flagged as "pre-qualified" or offering a personal line of credit as overdraft protection because your account was in an overdraft status? Well, I have, and it can be overwhelming when you do not understand banking terminology.

Truthfully speaking, banks can be our best friend, especially if we don't have the capital to fund our own expenses (house, car, loans for school, etc.), but, as with any other organization, they are in the business to make money. Although, they may persuade you in to thinking you do need a credit card or it's the "right time to buy a house", know that whatever product you do decide to take advantage of, they are profiting from it in some way.

During my years in the banking industry, I've encountered many sales and product pitches of getting consumers to fall victim to banking tactics. Activities such as coercing the consumer into a product or service they did not need to grow the business to maximize shareholders' wealth. This activity has always saddened me because, I too have fallen prey to these tactics.

Besides learning how to budget, educating yourself about the world of banking is critical because this is the place where your money is stored until you decide to use it. Take the terms "pre-qualified" and "pre-approved" for example. Some consumers do not understand the difference. A pre-qualifying loan/line of credit means that the lender simply "believes" the applicant is a potential good borrower based on the little information provided. A pre-approved loan/line of credit means that the lender did a thorough credit check on the consumer. Tax returns, bank statements, and other important documents were reviewed to determine the exact amount the consumer is eligible to receive.

Placing blame on the banks for our negative banking behaviors is not beneficial, when truthfully it is our own responsibility to educate ourselves about what happens if we apply for credit, whether or not it is smart to apply for a mortgage, and when to use our debit or credit cards.

When you learn the basics of budgeting and begin to build financially, you should take advantage of some products (not loans) that banks and financial institutions have to offer. Most of us only know about basic checking and savings accounts, but there are many other products available that you should use to your advantage. Before choosing an account, research all the products and services available on their website or stop in to have a face-to face discussion with a bank representative. Your mission should be to build a long-lasting healthy relationship with a financial institution that you can trust. You want the advantage of competitive interest rates, products and services available for every stage of your life, and competent representatives with great business practices.

Bank products you should use to your advantage:

- **Interest-bearing checking accounts and high-yield savings accounts**

  Interest-bearing checking and high-yield savings accounts generally offer higher interest rates compared to regular checking and savings accounts. This means that you will earn more interest income than regular checking and savings accounts. The more money you keep in the accounts, the more "free money" you will receive.

- **Online savings accounts**

  Online savings accounts operate the same as regular savings accounts. The only difference is that the account is strictly online. The advantage of online savings accounts is that the interest rates are relatively higher. Of course, obtaining the funds can take much longer than if you were to have a savings account at a local bank. An online savings account is a great account to have as your emergency savings (assuming you follow the checking and savings account strategy in Chapter 3).

- **Young savers account**

  Young savers accounts (also called a child savings account) are accounts for minors, typically 13 years old or younger. Young savers accounts can help children develop money management skills and teach them how to save money. This account can be used to help save for any money earned, Christmas expenses, or back-to-school shopping. Most young savers accounts are free, but it may require an initial deposit just like the other accounts listed.

- **Sign-up bonuses**

  When choosing a new bank, look to see if they have any sign-up bonuses that offer anywhere from $100.00 - $500.00, just for opening a new account. Typically, these sort of cash incentive flyer advertisements arrive in the mail. They may also be available online. Sign-up bonuses are a great way to establish a new relationship and get FREE money!

- **Keep the change program (round up to save program)**

  When you make purchases, the keep the change program will round your total to the nearest dollar and deposit any remaining funds into a savings account associated with the checking account. Remember, small savings = big savings. You will be surprised at how much you save in "loose" change. There is also a financial app called Acorns that does this as well.

- **Money market account**

  A money market account is a type of savings account, but functions like a checking account. You can write checks and withdraw funds using a debit card. These accounts also have higher interest rates compared to regular savings accounts too. More interest income for you!

- **Certificates of deposit**

  Certificates of Deposits are also known as a CD account. These accounts typically offer higher interest rates compared to high-yield savings and money market accounts. With certificate of deposit accounts, you can deposit a certain amount of money for a specific amount of time and when the term is completed, you will earn the interest. With this account, the money must be kept in the account or you will be penalized (money will be withheld from you) for withdrawing the funds too early. It's important to note that the longer the term, the higher the interest rate of return will be.

- **Individual retirement account**

  An Individual Retirement Account (IRA), is a great alternative to help save for retirement. An IRA account is a tax-advantage account that allows you to save for retirement tax-free or on a tax-deferred basis. With this account, you make contributions (there is a maximum contribution limit) and watch your retirement savings grow. There are several types of IRA's so do your research to determine which one is right for you.

- **Investment accounts**

  Investment accounts typically offer higher returns than the accounts listed previously. Please note that these are investment accounts, so it comes with investment risk. Once you begin to build financially, your ultimate goal should be to invest. This is just one way to become wealthy!

  Standard brokerage account: Brokerage accounts are accounts that contain stocks, bonds, and other financial instruments that help grow your personal net worth. There are special investment advisors (also known as financial advisors) that handle these accounts. You can also set up your IRA as an investment account too (you will earn more with an investment IRA versus a bank IRA). For standard brokerage accounts, the greater the risk, the greater the return. This means the more you invest, the more money you will receive or lose based on the stock market.

  529 college savings plan: A 529 college savings plan is a plan that helps to pay for college expenses at any qualified college or university nationwide. The funds grow tax free and withdrawals are not taxable (withdraws MUST be used for college expenses).

This is a great way to save for books, computers, supplies, and other qualifying college expenses that drain your wallet. I recommend opening this account as early as possible. The earlier you save, the more you will earn over time.

Coverdell education savings account: A Coverdell education savings account (Coverdell ESA) is an account similar to a 529 college savings plan, but it is generally used for grades K-12. This is because tax-free withdrawals on 529 college savings plans for grades K-12 are limited. This investment account is great for those who have children in private school.

UGMA/UTMA: (Uniform Gifts to Minors Act, Uniform Transfers to Minors Act) Custodial accounts set up by parents to help minors save money and invest. The custodian (adult) manages the account until the child is no longer a minor. This account is great to help build generational wealth.

The difference between a bank and a credit union

Banks are considered for-profit organizations, which means they generate profits to build capital to maximize shareholders' wealth (keep investors happy). Compared to credit unions, they tend to have more products available and their technical features are more advanced.

Credit unions are not-for-profit organizations which means their profits are generally giving back in the form of higher interest rates on savings accounts, lower interest rates on loans, and lower fees (keep members happy). Compared to a bank, it could be hard to open an account because they have more restrictions in terms of membership.

Do your research to determine which financial institution is best suited for you. Although a credit union may sound better because of higher interest rates on savings accounts, it could be hard to move money around because of their technical features. Although banks generally have more locations, they may persuade you to open additional accounts to increase profits.

In addition to the accounts listed, there are a few other tips I want to share, in terms of banking.

- **Avoid unnecessary fees**

  Research have shown that banks profit billions of dollar almost every year just in bank fees. Bank fees are the most common and unnecessary fees that should be avoided. Be sure to follow all account guidelines. Read the guidelines thoroughly. Some accounts require a direct deposit to avoid a maintenance fee. Student accounts are only free for a few years before it's converted to a regular checking or savings account. Never give the bank free money! Below is a list of bank fees you should be aware of.

  - **Maintenance fee-** fee charged for not following account guidelines. (ex. maintaining a balance of $500 or more daily, direct deposit of $250 or higher)

- **Nonsufficient funds (NSF) fee-** fee charged for not having enough money to cover the transaction(s). The item is unpaid with a NSF fee. (ex. Bounced check)
- **Overdraft fee-** fee charged for not having enough money to cover the transaction(s). The item is paid with an overdraft fee. (ex. Courtesy pay)
- **Foreign transaction charge-** fee charged for making a foreign purchase (non -US purchase) using a US bank card.
- **Stop payment fee-** fee charged for placing a hold on a check. (stopping a check from processing)
- **Inactive account fee-** fee charged for not having any account activity for an extended period of time, typically 12 months or longer.
- **Early account closing fee-** fee charged for closing an account before its probationary period.
- **Wire transfer fee-** fee charged for transferring money from one bank account to another electronically.
- **Paper statement fee/Copy statement fee-** fee charged for receiving paper statements of monthly transactions each month.
- **Debit card replacement fee-**fee charged for a lost or stolen debit card.
- **Check image service fee-**fee charged for obtaining copies of checks cashed.
- **Cashier's check/ Money order fee-** fee charged for purchasing a money order or cashier's check.
- **ATM fee (surcharge)-**fee charged for using another financial institutions ATM. (Search to see if your financial institution is a part of the Allpoint network to waive any surcharge fees)

- **Beware of inactive accounts**

After a period of no activity (usually a few years), any unused accounts become dormant and the funds are classified as unclaimed property. This is why you see many "unclaimed cash" advertisements or news articles. Never leave an account unattended. Your account could become fully depleted because of fees. It's your money, never let the state take it.

- **Don't use overdraft protection as your emergency fund**

Don't allow the bank to let your debit card go through for purchases you can't afford. You will most likely get charged a $35 overdraft fee for each transaction that will hurt your budget. To avoid this, opt-out of this service.

Financial institutions do offer overdraft protection as a credit account. I don't recommend this because the interest rate is relatively high, usually around 18% or higher. This means that you will have to pay interest just for small purchases. There are situations where unexpected circumstances do occur that could cause you to spend more than you have available, but this is why you are saving. This is why it is important to minimize expenses and focus on building your emergency fund.

Tip: Do not link your credit card as overdraft protection! This is just another way to add on more debt and interest charges in the long run.

- **Ask for fees to be waived**

  Let's face it, mistakes happen. Bills on autopay may come out twice or you accidentally used your bill bank account to pay for a personal expense that caused the account to go negative. Your banks ATM was down and you had to use a foreign ATM instead. In situations like this, I recommend contacting your financial institution and ask for the fee to be waived. Explain the situation and ask if there is something they could do to assist. Sometimes financial institutions are very generous and waive fees as a courtesy. An adjustment may not happen every time, especially if you always have these fees added to your account because of careless activity, but it never hurts to just ask.

- **Be mindful of joint accounts**

  It doesn't matter who puts the most into the account or who takes the most out of the account. With joint accounts, each party is held responsible. Be mindful that it is often hard to get your name removed from a joint account. With joint accounts, open it with someone you can trust.

- **Read the terms and conditions**

  ALWAYS read the terms and conditions. Don't bypass the fine print, as it has important information that you need to know. Read everything before leaving the bank. Bankers have been known to open accounts to reap larger commissions or add on additional products or services that you do not need. Make sure you understand the type of account(s) you are opening. Never walk away without knowing what is in your name and always ASK QUESTIONS!

- **Understand your interest rate**

  Interest rates create interest income. It also determines how much extra we have to pay for loans and other credit accounts. When applying for a loan or considering a new savings account, always compare interest rates.

  The words annual percentage rate (APR) and annual percentage yield (APY) are used interchangeably in the financial world. Generally, you will see the term APR used for loans and the term APY used when discussing savings accounts. Here's why:

  The APY includes how often interest is applied to your balance. It includes compound interest (interest on top of interest), making it your true rate. The APY (your true rate) is always higher than the APR when compounded daily or monthly. This is why lenders typically give you the APR on loans because they want to display the lower rate but give you the APY on savings accounts because they want to display the higher rate.

  Suggestion: When you do decide that you want a new car loan, be sure to ask for the APY not the APR. When opening a new savings account, compare the best APY from different financial institutions to receive the most interest income over time.

- **Poor banking behaviors travel with you (generally up to five years)**

  Financial institutions have a way of communicating with each other through a system called ChexSystems. ChexSystems is a national consumer reporting agency that keeps track of negative banking behaviors. It keeps track of negative behaviors such as overdraft accounts, bounced checks, or failing to pay a fee. This makes it difficult to open a new account or try to establish a relationship with a new financial institution.

  Keep in mind that not all financial institutions use ChexSystems. These institutions are often referred to as second chance banks and can be found online or in your local area.

- **Banking violation - "regulation d" – constant withdrawals from your savings account**

  Regulation D limits the use of withdrawing or transferring funds from your savings account per statement cycle. Regulation D, often referred to as Reg D, is one of the ways the bank maintains its reserve requirements and also keeps you from withdrawing or transferring too many times.

  Violating Regulation D comes with fees. This fee is known as a withdrawal limit fee. The fee is usually between $5.00-$20.00. Also, with this regulation, financial institutions can convert your savings account to an interest bearing account (checking account) if there are too many violations over the course of time.

- **Every offer is not a great offer**

  Every offer is not a great offer, just because it has the words "0%", "cash back", "no payment down" or "no fees", associated with it. These words may seem good, however, the type of product may not benefit your current financial situation. Do extensive research to find out exactly how the offer will benefit you. Remember, never walk away without knowing what is in your name. Read the terms and conditions thoroughly. Always ask questions.

CHAPTER 9

HOW TO KEEP A HANDLE ON DAILY PERSONAL SPENDING

Personal spending!

We often do very well with saving and organizing our finances on paper, but when it comes to personal spending, it almost never goes as planned. Have you ever made a goal to not buy clothes for a month or so and failed? What about dining and entertainment costs? How many times have you said you wouldn't go out with friends but ended up at the party anyways?

After years of understanding how to make my budget work for me, I came to realize that you don't necessarily have to deprive yourself of the things you love. That will only force you to want the item(s) even more. If shopping is one of your hobbies, you can't just wake up and decide you are not going to do it anymore because eventually you will again. And most likely, you will end up spending more to compensate for all the other times that you didn't get what you wanted. YOU CAN'T FOOL YOUR OWN SELF!

Instead of fully depriving yourself, focus on trying to spend money in moderation. Opposed to spending $100.00 a week on clothes, try to minimize the amount to $50.00 then eventually to only $10.00 – $20.00 a week. When it comes to wants, we have to learn how to control our desires. There is nothing wrong with spending money on wants, however, we have to learn how to limit ourselves.

Personal spending can make or break your finances. Below, I will provide several tips to help with everyday spending.

- Break down your personal spending funds. Allocate a certain amount for clothes, entertainment and other personal spending items per paycheck/per month. Always set a limit to avoid overspending.

- Track daily spending. Get into the habit or routine in the morning of checking your personal bank account to know what you have available and how much you've spent. You should make it a habit to track your expenses. Buy a notebook or planner to track spending. Use the budgeting worksheet for tracking purposes. If you love Excel, Microsoft Office provides several budgeting tracker worksheets that you can use. In addition to this, there are several apps that provide budgeting trackers. Every Dollar, Clarity Money, and Good Budget are great apps to use.

- Include fast food and dining costs as part of your food budget, not just for groceries.

- Always look and ask for discounts. Never pay the full price if you can avoid it.

- Don't compete with gifts. Don't feel obligated to buy an expensive gift just because someone buys you something nice. Remember, you are on a budget. You are focusing on your financial goals. Expensive gifts only hold you back from achieving financial success. And remember, debt should not be used to fund daily activities. If you have to purchase a gift on credit, it is not a gift anymore, it is a financial burden.

Be mindful of day-to-day purchases that drain your wallet. Examples:

- ➢ Eating out everyday
- ➢ Vending machines
- ➢ Lottery tickets
- ➢ Couponing too much (buying excessively just because its inexpensive)
- ➢ Partying every weekend
- ➢ Weekly brunch or lunch with friends and family often
- ➢ Driving unnecessary
- ➢ Purchasing cheap gas that doesn't last long
- ➢ Buying coffee every morning
- ➢ Unnecessary pampering and grooming services
- ➢ Unnecessary fees (ex. bank fees)
- ➢ $0.99-$5.00 purchases
- ➢ Parking meters (get a parking pass if you can instead)

- Write out a list before shopping. Avoid spending money on things you don't need and already have at home.

- Choose quality products. It's better to spend a little more on quality that will last versus buying the same cheap thing repeatedly. Also, consider purchasing protection and warranty plans for household appliances and electronics.

- Beware of the decoy marketing strategy

Small coffee: $5.00   Medium coffee: $5.55   Large coffee: $5.95

The decoy strategy (also called the decoy effect or decoy pricing) is a strategy that many companies use to persuade you to buy the larger item. They set the smallest item price very high to make it seem like you are getting a better deal but, in reality, they are only profiting more from the sale.

Remember small savings equals big savings. Save loose change as much as you can.

- Stay at home. You don't have to attend every event that you are invited to. Surround yourself with people who are going to motivate you for achieving financial success. It's okay to say, "No thanks, I'm on a budget!"

- Say no to "window shopping". This helps to avoid impulse buying.

- Remove debit and credit cards from websites. This helps with impulse buying too.

- To minimize clothes and shoes expenses, consider buying clothes during off seasons. Buy summer clothes in the winter and winter clothes in the summer. And remember, you don't need a new outfit for EVERY occasion. Check your closet before purchasing something new all the time.

- Don't let holidays, birthdays, graduations, and anniversaries distract you from achieving your financial goals. Keep track of these expenses with your yearly expense worksheet. Set a limit and stick to it.

- Follow the 7-day rule. Refer back to Chapter 3 on the 7-day rule to avoid impulse buying. If you want something (new outfit, shoes, etc.) wait 7 days and if you still want it, see if your budget will allow you to purchase it. The objective here is to change your mind about purchasing that particular item.

- Look for liquidation and going out of business sales
Only get what you NEED. Sometimes we can get caught up on the word "sale", that we forget that although we are saving, we are also spending. Liquidation and going out of business sales are great opportunities to get what you need at a discounted cost, but set a budget for this.

- Only take out what you need from the ATM.

- Use gift cards that you've received or turn any unused gift card(s) into cash (card cash, card pool, or visit a gift card exchange kiosk).

- Shift your mindset. Focus on purchasing things that appreciate (increase) the value of your money versus depreciate (decrease) the value of your money over time.

- Understand cheap versus frugal when it comes to daily spending. A cheap individual is someone who purchases items just because it is inexpensive. Their main focus is to get the best deal out of every transaction. A frugal person, on the other hand, is one who not only shops for the best deal, but also considers quality and value. Although it is important to shop for the best deals, never buy items "just because". Always review your budget and set limits with every purchase, no matter the cost.

CHAPTER 10

ADDITIONAL INFORMATION - PERSONAL FINANCE

I want to provide you with more! More savings, more budgeting tips, and more knowledge of eliminating debt, as this should be your first financial goal. As stated previously, once you build this foundation, then you will be able to achieve greater financial success.

The additional tips and strategies presented below provides knowledge of personal finance that you should become aware of:

- **Practice having a frugal lifestyle**

    Do you know that Warren Buffett, one of the richest men in the world, would spend $3.00 for breakfast each morning on his way to work, still lives in the same house since 1958, and uses coupons? I read an article and watched a documentary about him several years ago and I was shocked. This was an amazing discovery.

    Just because you have more money to spend, doesn't mean you should. Increase income doesn't mean to increase debt and expenses. It defeats the purpose.

- **Check your progress**

    Try not to get so caught up in budgeting, eliminating debt, and saving, that your lose sight of how WELL you are actually doing. Set your own goals and monitor your progress. Create a "goals accomplished worksheet". This is a great motivation tactic, especially when you begin to see big results.

- **Stay in your own financial lane**

    Never compare your financial journey or progress to anyone. Financial success is not defined by "who finishes first" or "who achieves the most" in a specific period of time. Accomplishing goals is a marathon, not a sprint. It takes time to eliminate bad financial habits and save, especially if this is your first time.

- **Don't allow limited income to "limit you" from learning the importance of budgeting**

  When it comes to budgeting, many individuals think that just because they make less than the average person, they are not equipped to budget. It doesn't matter if you earn $30,000.00 a year or $100,000.00. If you don't know how to manage money properly, you will always end up with financial struggles. Learn to manage smaller income so when your income does increase, you will know how to manage it.

- **Check your bills regularly**

  Companies sometimes have the tendency of raising fees without proper notification. It doesn't matter if it's a $5 increase or a $10 increase, an increase is an increase. Call and ask questions. Ask why the bill increased. See if there is anyway the bill can be decreased. The mission is to minimize expenses as much as possible.

- **Pay attention to financial and economic trends**

  Economic fluctuations affect your well-being, so it's imperative that you understand and are up to date with current financial events. Here are a few current financial events that I have researched that you should be aware of:

  - When interest rates in the economy increase or decrease, it affects the interest rates on credit cards, mortgage rates, consumer spending, and savings accounts, just to name a few things. For example, when interest rates increase, you earn more interest income on savings accounts, but the cost of borrowing increases.

  - In 2018, tax liens and civil judgements were removed from credit reports by the credit bureaus (Equifax, Experian, TransUnion) which helped to boost consumer credit scores.

  - The IRS raised the cap on 401(k) contributions from $18,000.00 in 2017 to $19,500.00 in 2021. This can help to reduce adjusted gross income/taxable income and help save more for retirement.

  - The new Tax Cuts and Jobs Act, which was passed at the end of 2017, affected both individual and business taxes tremendously. Individuals saw a difference on things such as higher standard deductions and new marginal tax rate brackets. The corporate tax rate for businesses changed as well.

  - The future for social security retirement benefits remain uncertain as many financial strategists predict that the social security trust fund will become exhausted by 2034-2035. With this prediction, millennials and generations born after will have to formulate other ways to generate income after retirement. Social security benefits will not completely disappear, but total benefits will be reduced. (Less will be paid out year by year)

As stated in the beginning, you don't have to be a financial expert, but you do need to understand basic financial literacy. The world has evolved providing us with more access to general knowledge. The next time you see an article about credit, but unsure of some of the terminology, look it up. Search for other articles on that same topic. You will be pleasantly surprised about how much you will learn about finance that goes well beyond the topics of budgeting, saving, and eliminating debt.

- Use the financial apps that are available on your smart phone. The good thing about this is that most of the apps are FREE! Take advantage of it today.

- In addition to car and home insurance, get life insurance too.
  Death can be very cumbersome for the family members who have to handle the business affairs once you have passed. Having life insurance will help your loved ones tremendously. Get life insurance while you are younger. The younger and healthier you are, the lower your payments will be. If your employer offers life insurance, take advantage of that option too.

- Avoid payday loans and other high interest loans that increase your monthly expenses because of high interest payments.

- Be careful of predatory lending. Predatory lending is an unfair, unethical, or misleading loan a borrower gets approved for that ultimately benefits the lender. Extremely high-interest rates and numerous fees are usually the first signs of predatory lending. If it is your first time buying a car or home, read all documents thoroughly. Never rush to sign papers. Look for the APY (your true rate), and not the advertised APR. Ensure the loan is one that will fit into your budget. Don't forget the financial rules of thumb!

- Take advantage of any employer perks and fringe benefits such as health savings accounts, flexible spending accounts, 401(k) plans, and any educational programs.

- An IRA account is not only for adults. If you have a child who earns income from a qualified source, they can open an IRA account as well. This is will help grow their personal finances more than a traditional savings account. It is a great way to jumpstart a better life financially.

Know your credit score rating

Credit is important because it determines your creditworthiness. It determines how responsible you are at handling financial obligations, so it is imperative that you learn to manage your money now so that your will be able to generate and maintain a high credit score in the future.

Approximately 90% of lenders use what's called your FICO score (created by the Fair Isaac Corporation) to determine your credit risk. One important element of credit is understanding the five factors that make up your FICO credit score. The five factors that make up your FICO credit score are:

1. Number of on-time payments: makes up 35% of your credit score

2. Credit utilization ratio: makes up 30% of your credit score (the percentage of revolving credit being used)

3. Length of credit history: makes up 15% of your credit score

4. Credit mix (number of accounts): makes up 10% of your credit score

5. Number of hard inquiries: makes up 10% of your credit score

Understanding these five factors is important because it determines how high or low your credit score will be. Please be advised that a missed payment can drop your credit score by up to 50 points. Having a high credit utilization ratio (ex. carrying a high credit card balance) can drop your credit score by up to 100 points. Also, applying for too many credit accounts over a short period of time can drastically lower your credit score too. Take some time getting to know these five factors to improve and maintain a high credit score.

- **Tips to help build and improve your credit score rating**
  In addition to understanding the five factors that make up your credit score and creating strategies to eliminate debt, there are many other ways to help build and improve your credit score rating. Understanding the five factors and the tips below has personally helped me to increase my credit score rating.

  1. Dispute and correct any negative items on your credit report. Ensure the information shown is indeed accurate.

  2. Apply for a credit builder loan (highly recommended-helps to save and build/improve credit at the same time).

  3. Keep your credit utilization ratio at 30% or lower. (Only use up to 30% of the available limit on your credit cards. For best results, pay the full statement balance by the due date.)

  4. New credit laws implemented. For example, the removal of tax liens by the credit bureaus in 2018 helped to boost consumers' credit scores.

  5. Keep credit cards active and open. Closing a credit card can potentially increase your credit utilization ratio, decrease your credit mix (number of accounts), and decrease your length of credit history. All of these factors can negatively affect your credit score.

- **Celebrate your financial successes!** Financial success doesn't have to be brutal, it's okay to be proud of yourself for a job well done.

Consider these strategies and you will become financially stable in no time!

AFTERWORD:

MAKE GIVING A PART OF YOUR FINANCIAL GOALS

The content of this message is not to lecture you about giving. I'm not here to tell you that it is mandatory to give, but I will say that it should always be a part of your financial goals. An important part to becoming financially successful is giving.

You see, I understood the concept of reaping and sowing, but never fully "understood" what it truly meant until a few years ago. For so long I would hear scriptures about giving. Scriptures such as 2 Corinthians 9:6 which states *"whoever sows sparingly will also reap sparingly, and whoever sows bountifully will also reap bountifully"* and Acts 20:35 which states *"... it is more blessed to give than to receive"*.

Reflecting back on giving as part of my financial goals and if I am honest, I really thought the church organization just wanted money from me. Truthfully, I thought it was just a way for the church to get money out of people so the Pastor/Preacher could drive fancier cars. I found myself saying, "Oh great, they must also see an ATM sign on my forehead!"

In the last 2 years, I just kept studying and studying the word to get a better understanding of the scriptures and then it finally clicked in my head. For so many years, I wanted God to enlarge my territory, but I wasn't giving him anything to enlarge it with. If God couldn't trust me with the little I had, how could he trust me with more? How could I pray for more when I wasn't obedient with what I currently had? How could I expect a harvest, without planting a seed?

Like I stated previously, it took me awhile to realize this concept of reaping and sowing. I've always felt that it didn't matter if I sowed only a $1.00 or $2.00 because I would reap something in the end. What I can share with you is that since I'd become more obedient in my giving, I have experienced several supernatural things. Since I started giving more, I have been receiving more. For example, I have literally seen thousands of dollars' worth of medical bills turn into a refund check. Yes, You read correctly! I have witnessed issues with my transmission turn into there being no charge for the service. I restored what was loss in 2011 and gained so much more.

Sowing is not just about giving money all the time. It's about giving your time and your heart too. It's about serving and giving back to those that are in need. We are all born with a specific talent that should be sown into others. It's important that we sow seeds of the fruits of the spirt into the lives of others. If you truly have nothing to give, seek guidance and look for ways to give differently. Find what purpose you serve and help individuals with that gift. We are all connected to each other spiritually, so if we aren't obedient, it will not only hurt you but the people who are connected to you too. And believe me when I say this, you never know who is on the other side ready to give you that financial breakthrough you so desperately want to have!

Reaping has more to do with just receiving monetary gain as well. In the past two years, I have uncovered many hidden talents that I never knew I had! Battles that I once worried about in the past diminished and became nonexistent. I find more peace in my life now. Look at this, never in my life would I have thought I could be an author!

There are so many benefits when giving back. Think of all the famous people that stress the importance of giving. There are many philanthropists who provide guidance of how and why it is important to give. Think about someone you know personally that gives freely of themselves of whatever they have. I'm pretty sure, they are in the process of receiving their blessings for being a giver.

Gifting of monetary value doesn't just have to be giving to a church. There are many charities and non-profit organizations that you can sow into. There are many individuals who donate to different organizations to help a cause. There are some people who struggle to find a place to eat and rest their head at night, but your generosity can help to make their situation a bit easier for them momentarily.

I know, in the beginning, I talked about learning to say no and that it's okay to be selfish. However, sowing and reaping are completely different from giving and enabling. Giving for a purpose is not the same as giving because someone is not responsible or careless with their money, which led them to their current way of life. Giving promotes abundance. Planting financial seeds will help to reap a financial harvest.

You should think of sowing as paying yourself first. If you want to achieve success for yourself, then you need to invest in yourself. Give what's in your heart to give. Think about what Proverbs 11:24 says- *"Give freely and become more wealthy; be stingy and lose everything."*

Always remember…

> **"WHEN YOU LEARN TO BE AN INFLUENCE AND GIVE, THE AFFLUENCE WILL FOLLOW!"**

Good Luck on your financial journey!

NOTES

ABOUT THE AUTHOR

Alicia Gage, a certified financial education instructor, financial coach, and accountant, currently resides in Charleston, SC. Alicia holds a bachelor's and master's degree in finance. She enjoys the ability to help others. At the age of 30, Alicia went on a personal journey to discover her purpose and created Alicia's Financial Corner, an organization designed to help individuals build a better relationship with money through budgeting, saving, debt elimination, and credit education. Alicia is highly motivated by the word success. Despite adversity, Alicia continues to educate herself daily and uses previous knowledge learned in her professional experience to empower others on the importance of financial literacy.

Website: www.aliciasfinancialcorner.com
Email: aliciasfinancialcorner@gmail.com
Facebook: Alicia's Financial Corner LLC
Instagram: Aliciasfinancialcorner

www.ingramcontent.com/pod-product-compliance
Lightning Source LLC
Chambersburg PA
CBHW051228200326
41519CB00025B/7297